"Faith Blatchford's *Winning the Battle for the Night* is wonderfully practical, brilliantly insightful and sure to inspire the reader to reconnect with God's purpose for sleep—communion and rest. Our capacity to fellowship with God is sometimes stronger in the night than in the day, when we often have so many distractions. He longs to communicate with us through the dream realm. He deposits things in our hearts and minds while we sleep that we wouldn't be able to process while awake. We can position ourselves for this, as a yielded imagination becomes a sanctified imagination, and a sanctified imagination is positioned for visions and dreams. This is for everyone!"

Bill Johnson, Bethel Church, Redding, California;
author, *When Heaven Invades Earth*, *God Is Good*
and *The Power That Changes the World*

"I love this book. I've read many books on dreams, but Faith Blatchford's story and unique insights caught me up in wonder and ignited hunger to be saturated in the last-days language of the Holy Spirit. This book will provoke you to take the dream seriously and act on it. In so doing you will become a shaper of history. I've been in the dream stream for years, but this book put a further hook in my heart. I can no longer say, "It was just a dream." It was the roar of the Lord! Read it and find your night wings."

Lou Engle, co-founder, TheCall

"I am excited about this book. Faith does an excellent job of explaining how sleep can become our friend to help us grow spiritually. You will find this book a great help as you yourself learn the importance of dreams and sleep not for just yourself but for your whole family. Great job, Faith!"

Beni Johnson, author, *Healthy and Free*
and *The Happy Intercessor*

"Faith Blatchford's *Winning the Battle for the Night* is a beautifully written book that helps us prepare our hearts to find sweet sleep so that we can dream with God."

Linda Evans Shepherd, author, *Winning Your Daily Spiritual Battles*

"Faith Blatchford has been my friend for more than thirty years. The word *passionate* describes her well. She is also challenging, original, witty and imaginative in her writing. *Winning the Battle for the Night* captivated me and encouraged me anew to listen to God—indeed to ask Him for dreams. Faith Blatchford challenges me deeply, but kindly and honestly. This unique book will help countless thousands."

Pam Rosewell Moore, executive director, Pam Rosewell Moore Ministries

"Wow! Insightful, helpful, a joy to read. While I've read books on dream interpretation, I have not come across one that helps remove the barriers to dreaming. Faith explores the hindrances that keep us from communing with God in the night hours. What a great read."

Gwen Gibson, associate pastor, Hope Center, HRock Church

"Increasingly, people report sleep problems, which lead to poor physical and mental well-being. *Winning the Battle for the Night* explores the importance of sleep, giving practical steps to restore God's nighttime gift. It will empower you to value and experience good sleep, thus improving health, performance, wisdom and God-given creativity."

Dr. Michelle A. Miller, Warwick Medical School, University of Warwick

"This is a powerful guide for anyone who has struggled with sleep problems, and the first book I've seen that so clearly explains the spiritual science behind sleep. Faith Blatchford arms you with relevant and practical information about the physiological, psychological and spiritual roots to sleeplessness. Her insights will give you hope and help you reclaim God's design for rejuvenation and revelation through sleep."

Margaret Nagib, Psy.D., clinical psychologist,
Timberline Knolls Residential Treatment Center;
founder, The Dunamis Project

"I never knew how significant sleep and a healthy dream life were until reading *Winning the Battle for the Night*. I was immediately drawn into the book by the real-life stories from both the author and well-known historical figures. I greatly appreciated Faith Blatchford's ability to clearly combine teaching, research, practical application and personal learning and turn this into a personal guide and reference book that I will use and recommend for the rest of my night life!"

Andy Mason, author, *God with You at Work*
and *Dream Culture: Bringing Dreams to Life*;
director, Heaven in Business,
www.heaveninbusiness.com

"In my career as a medical doctor, I have clearly understood the challenges caused by poor sleep. Faith Blatchford helpfully addresses the subject from different angles, not only aiding understanding but also offering practical solutions. Accessing practical help on the physical issues, finding the peace of God, which can guard our hearts and minds, and interacting on a spiritual level with the Prince of Peace all combine in *Winning the Battle for the Night*."

Peter Carter, M.D., family practioner in the U.K.;
director, Eastgate, www.eastgate.org.uk;
author, *Unwrapping Lazarus*

"Reading this has reminded me of the importance of adequate sleep and rest from both a biblical and a medical perspective. This excellent scholarly work integrates key Scriptures with evidence-based medical practice to address sleep and rest deprivation. Anyone desiring to put into practice the truths found within the pages of this book will find a deeper, richer meaning with which to live their lives."

Brenda B. Jones, Ph.D., assistant professor of nursing,
Lee University

"This generation has more distractions from sleep than any generation before. Faith does an excellent job of explaining the importance of sleep and dreams but also gives so much encouragement in telling us how much God wants to give us dreams. *Winning the Battle for the Night* will bring a fresh confidence in God's design for sleep and dreams and challenge you to contend for more!"

Kim Walker-Smith, Jesus Culture

WINNING THE
BATTLE
FOR THE
NIGHT

WINNING THE
BATTLE
FOR THE
NIGHT

God's Plan for Sleep, Dreams and Revelation

FAITH D. BLATCHFORD

Chosen

a division of Baker Publishing Group
Minneapolis, Minnesota

© 2017 by Age to Come

Published by Chosen Books
11400 Hampshire Avenue South
Bloomington, Minnesota 55438
www.chosenbooks.com

Chosen Books is a division of
Baker Publishing Group, Grand Rapids, Michigan

Printed in the United States of America

ISBN 978-0-8007-9818-5

Library of Congress Control Number: 2017936786

Cover design by LOOK Design Studio

17 18 19 20 21 22 23   7 6 5 4 3 2 1

This book is dedicated to my dreaming friends,
whose dreams from God at night
stirred my desire for similar experiences.
Without you, my life would not have been changed and this book
would not have been written.

CONTENTS

FOREWORD

I love all the areas of freedom Faith Blatchford has claimed for so many people. Here comes another one! The number of lives that are totally disrupted over the issue of sleep deprivation is stunning. We must build solutions to this chronic problem that are rooted in truth and actually help people stay free. In thirty years of working with people, I have learned that many of the problems in life are massively exacerbated by poor sleep habits.

The number of life struggles that are connected to sleep issues is staggering: anxiety, depression, inability to focus, lack of sex drive, accidents, heart problems, poor judgment and hopelessness, to name a few. If we leave the issue of sleep unaddressed, we will chase all kinds of solutions that don't get to what we need.

Hopelessness is a fruit that comes from being unable to find a solution to a personal issue permeating our daily life. I have heard several of my friends say something that I believe applies here: "Any area in our life where we are hopeless exposes a place where we are believing a lie." I agree with this conclusion. When we apply a set of truths to our life, therefore, the results are life, freedom and happiness.

Faith's prophetic gift and her high level of compassion make her the perfect person to write this book. With insights on how people function and a tender heart toward God, she is able to pull years of experience together to help with a common and plaguing issue in our society today. She is leading people right out of their nightmares and into their dreams. This book will be a set of keys to those who have been held in the darkness of hopelessness and confusion for far too long. I am happy to see this work finally released.

God Bless,
Danny Silk, author, *Keep Your Love On*,
Loving Our Kids on Purpose,
Culture of Honor and *Powerful and Free*

ACKNOWLEDGMENTS

Helen Keller said, "Alone we can do so little; together we can do so much." This truth applies to the writing of this book, as well as to every other area of my life. The words *thank you*, though meaningful, are not powerful enough to express to those listed below how much I appreciate their contribution to this book. For now, however, those words will have to suffice for the four teams involved in this project.

First and foremost, I thank God for His inspiration and revelation for this book, and I thank the Holy Spirit for collaborating in the writing process.

Thank you to the prayer team, which included Marla and her team, and also David, Beryl, James, Carol, Ginger, Bob, John, Judy, Erin, Jon, Joanna, Carl, Steve, Dawna, Cory, Bill, Diane, Alline, Tom, Kim, Ruthann, James, Jenny, Deborah, Chuck, Nancy, Brenda, Tracy, Sally, Maureen, Kathy, Beaver, Jen, Pete, Ginny, Hugh, Liz, Stuart, Laurie, Anna, Tim, Jen, Mina, Rev22, Alun and Donna.

Many thanks to the working team of Pam Spinosi, Dr. Jennifer Jones and Patty Shannon.

And finally, thank you to Jane Campbell of Chosen Books and the entire publishing team of Baker Publishing Group and Chosen Books.

What If?

And being warned by God in a dream,
he turned aside into the region of Galilee.
Matthew 2:22

I love Christmas! Yes, I keep my tree up all year long. No, it is not a miracle tree; it is wrought iron, filled with elephant ornaments of every size, shape and color, part of a lifelong elephant collection. A five-foot stuffed Santa, holding a monkey suited in jolly green, presides in the living room, as he should in his role as Father Christmas. In a prominent spot on an antique chest in another corner is a Nativity scene. The delicately carved Jesus looks up from the tiny cradle, attended by Mary, Joseph, the three wise men, several shepherd boys, a few of their sheep and of course the camels and an elephant. On top of the miniature stable's roof is a large angel representing one of the many in attendance that night. You may have grown up with one of these Nativity scenes yourself, and it is now in a box, ready to be displayed next Christmas.

That birthday, commemorated throughout the centuries in paintings, songs, books, plays, pageants all over the world, marked the beginning of a new era, a historic demarcation designated by the change on the calendar from BC (before Christ) to AD (in the year of our Lord). Mary and Joseph had some inkling of their son's significance, and the shepherds who responded to the angel choir's message had some awareness as well. It was the three wise men (called Magi), believers in the spirit world and the science of the stars, who knew that there was more than a star in the sky—there was a Star in the cradle. The birth of this baby terrified Herod, the emperor. He knew his kingdom was at risk because a new King had been born: Jesus, King of the Jews.

Warned in a Dream

Herod had heard the chatter about this special baby with the arrival in Jerusalem of the Magi who had journeyed from the East, following the unusual star that had appeared in the sky. He summoned these wise men to interrogate them about this star and its meaning. He then sent them on a mission to Bethlehem to locate this newborn, destined to be King. The scribes and Pharisees believed that Micah, the prophet, had foretold that the baby would be born in Bethlehem. The emperor's pretext in commissioning the Magi for this journey was to determine the baby's whereabouts in order to go himself to welcome and worship this Prince. God warned them in a dream not to return to Herod, so the three men went home by another route to avoid a second meeting with the emperor. Once they left, the angel of the Lord appeared to Joseph in a dream, instructing him to flee with Mary and Jesus to Egypt. They were to remain there until the angel returned with further instructions (see Matthew 2:3–15).

Meanwhile, Herod was furious, raging against the wise men who had disobeyed him by not returning with the information about the baby. He was so fearful of this child's existence that he ordered the massacre of every male child under two in Bethlehem and the surrounding area. Jeremiah had prophesied this horrific act over six hundred years before the slaughter (see Jeremiah 31:15). Joseph believed God communicated to men through angels, so he paid attention to the angel's warning.

But what if he had not obeyed? What if he had ignored the dream, thinking he had eaten too many lentils for dinner? What if he had discounted it, believing it was just a figment of his imagination? What if he had been so caught up with life in the natural, the new baby, the animals, the visitors, that he had not taken time to sleep so that he could *have* a dream? The answer to all those questions is that Herod's henchmen would have arrived at the stable and proceeded to carry out their assignment to kill all the babies. If it did not matter whether Joseph and the family stayed or not, God would not have sent the angel. The dream mattered. Christmas Day, rather than being a day of mourning over the death of a baby, has for centuries been a day of exceeding great joy, as heralded by the angels. So I keep my tree up.

"It Is Only a Dream"

President Abraham Lincoln had a dream a few days before his assassination. He shared it with his wife in the presence of his bodyguard, Ward Hill Lamon, who made notes of it and recounted it in a short biography, *Recollections of Abraham Lincoln 1847–1865*. This dream contained within it the possibility of an event that would have major historical impact, just as Joseph's dream had.

Here is Lincoln's recounting of the dream and his conversation about it with his wife. The president began the conversation by talking about dreams in the Bible:

"It seems strange how much there is in the Bible about dreams. There are, I think, some sixteen chapters in the Old Testament and four or five in the New in which dreams are mentioned; and there are many passages scattered throughout the book, which refer to visions. If we believe the Bible, we must accept the fact that in the old days God and His angels came to men in their sleep and made themselves known in dreams. Nowadays dreams are regarded as very foolish, and are seldom told, except by old women and by young men and maidens in love."

"Why, you look dreadfully solemn; do you believe in dreams?"

"I can't say that I do, but I had one the other night which has haunted me ever since."[1]

Lincoln then related to his wife how after the dream occurred, it seemed that every time he opened the Bible he encountered a dream or a vision wherever he looked. He told her that everywhere his eye fell upon a passage, it was strangely in keeping with his own thoughts about supernatural visitations, dreams, visions and the like.

This frightened Mrs. Lincoln, but not nearly so much as what he was about to add to his story. In his dream, he said, there was a deathlike stillness all around, and he heard a number of people weeping. Lincoln began moving from room to room in the White House to investigate. In every room he visited, invisible mourners broke the silence with pitiful sobbing, sounding as if their hearts would break. He kept going, determined to find the cause of the situation, until he entered the East Room. There, a sickening surprise awaited him—a catafalque supporting a corpse wrapped in funeral vestments, with the face covered and therefore out of view to him. All around, soldiers were stationed as guards, and a throng of people gazed mournfully upon the somber scene.

Lincoln then told his terrified wife the most distressing part of his dream:

"'Who is dead in the White House?' I demanded of one of the soldiers. 'The President,' was his answer; 'he was killed by an assassin!' Then came a loud burst of grief from the crowd, which awoke me from my dream. I slept no more that night; and although it was only a dream, I have been strangely annoyed by it ever since."

"That is horrid! I wish you had not told it. I am glad I don't believe in dreams, or I should be in terror from it from this time forth," said Mrs. Lincoln.

"Well," responded Mr. Lincoln, thoughtfully, "it is only a dream, Mary. Let us say no more about it, and try to forget it."[2]

In this case, rather than taking the dream as a warning from God, Lincoln viewed it as "only a dream." If he had believed God still spoke to people through dreams, as in Bible days, would he have added extra security measures? Would he have canceled his evening at Ford's Theatre? His bodyguard, Ward Hill Lamon, was out of town, but prior to his leaving, he had begged Lincoln to avoid going outside as much as possible and particularly to avoid events such as the theater. Whether it was the dream Lincoln had had or actual intelligence gathering, Mr. Lamon feared for Abe's safety. The president had told Lamon he would try his best to take the advice, but as history shows, his best did not include staying home on April 14, 1865, the night of his assassination at the theater.

Only speculation and active imagination can envision the answer to "what if" Lincoln had believed the dream was a warning from God and had sought Him for direction on how to respond. The United States had been torn apart by the Civil War for the first four years of his presidency. The war ended on April 9, 1865, and John Wilkes Booth shot Lincoln five days later. The words of his March 4, 1865, second inaugural address, which are carved on the walls of the Lincoln Memorial in Washington, D.C., give a glimpse of what the next four years of the Reconstruction would have looked like under his administration:

> With malice toward none; with charity for all; with firmness in the right, as God gives us to see the right, let us strive on to finish the work we are in; to bind up the nation's wounds; to care for him who shall have borne the battle, and for his widow, and his orphan—to do all which may achieve and cherish a just and a lasting peace, among ourselves, and with all nations.[3]

Without Lincoln's bold, courageous, God-fearing leadership, his vision of the Reconstruction never became a reality. Today, over 150 years later, the wounds of the Civil War are not completely healed. What a different nation we might be, if only Lincoln had not viewed his dream as "only a dream."

Mindsets Matter

These two dreams have historic impact even for us today. The difference between Joseph's response and Lincoln's reflects two different mindsets about dreams. I grew up with the biblical belief that God still gives people dreams at night, even though I had not had any that I remembered and had not heard anyone talk about a God dream. As I began my study about dreams, some of the articles written by Christian writers puzzled me. I first looked for articles about the subject in a respected encyclopedia, *The International Standard Bible Encyclopedia*. Because this was accepted in academic circles as being an authority on everything and anything biblical, I believed the information would be true to the Bible. What I read shocked me. Here are a few quotes:

> Dreams are abnormal and sometimes pathological. Sleep is a normal experience. Perfect and natural sleep should be without

dreams of any conscious occurrence. Perhaps psychologically there can be no such thing as perfectly dreamless sleep. Such a condition would probably be death itself.

The Bible, contrary to a notion perhaps too commonly held, attaches relatively little religious significance to dreams.

The New Testament gives still less place and importance to dreams than the Old Testament.

Whether God communicates directly or indirectly by dreams is still unsettled.[4]

Only later did I realize that popular theology stemming from the teachings of Thomas Aquinas, a thirteenth-century theologian, influenced the writer of this article on dreams. Aquinas was a brilliant thinker who came to the erroneous conclusion that our knowledge of God is limited to what our mind can comprehend or our five senses can experience. There was little room for any contact with God from a spiritual realm outside the body or mind. The long-term effect of this theology's insidious influence in the Western Christian mind has been skepticism and fear about any interaction with God through dreams. The result of this belief is tragic—we are robbed and God is silenced.

If you picked this book up because you suffer with insomnia, you may wonder what the theology of dreams has to do with your sleep issue. As you read, you will discover God's design of rest for the body, as well as His desire to instruct and inspire us as we sleep, equipping us for the day physically, mentally and spiritually. The devil's desire is to cut off this communication from God. He attempts to do this through the disruption of our sleep or through bad theology. My prayer is that as you receive this new information and revelation about God's plan for the night, your sleep will improve, your body and mind will be refreshed, and an environment will be created at night in which you receive dreams, revelation and songs from God.

Dealing with Doubt

Perhaps you are sensing a degree of doubt or even anxiety creeping into your thoughts as we explore the topic of God communicating with us as we sleep. I remember hearing people discount their dream by saying it was "a pizza dream." The idea that these dreams are just a result of what I ate seems to diminish the validity of all of them. Not only theology, but also current psychology has ignored dreams as having a legitimate influence. According to Robert Moss in *The Secret History of Dreaming*, psychology courses for undergraduates discount dreams as being irrelevant, a meaningless part of brain function.[5]

This quote from a *Medical News Today* article illustrates some of the current psychological and medical views on dreams: "Dreams are stories and images that our minds create while we sleep. They can be entertaining, fun, romantic, disturbing, frightening and sometimes bizarre."[6]

The article investigates the current research on dreams and looks at possible explanations and theories about why our minds invent these nightly musings. It is clear from the quoted description of dreams that the writer believes they all come from the same source—our own minds. The problem with this analysis of dreams is that we have no expectation of the influence from outside our mind and body of God as the initiator of dreams, or demons as the source of nightmares. As a result, we muzzle God and expose ourselves to the torment of unrestrained demons. Who knows how many dreams might have brought change through an invention, strategy or solution that could have benefited many more people than the dreamer, if only the dream had been valued.

Living in a world influenced by such views about the source and possible untrustworthiness or unimportance of dreams may cause us to approach this subject with a measure of skepticism. We don't need to allow what appears to be a lack of faith to stop us. We all have faith. We could not live if we did not exercise faith. Our capacity to function in life hinges on leaps of faith, some big, some small. Something as mundane as flopping into a comfortable chair is an exercise of faith as I sit down on it, trusting I won't end up on the floor. It was a choice I made about the solidness of the chair that gave me courage to put my weight on it. I can make the same decision to trust the soundness of God's Word and His desire to communicate with me through dreams via the Holy Spirit.

Regardless of what philosophers, theologians, scientists, agnostics, atheists and skeptics have postulated about God's interaction with man through dreams, God has the last word. Just because I decide God is not who He says He is does not change the truth about Him. What a different place the world would be if men and woman had spent as much time and money seeking to know God as they have in trying to disprove His existence. A negative focus in life in any area usually does not produce much benefit. I would much rather know what is than what isn't.

You may have been robbed of the truth about God without even realizing it. Before you read further, you might find it helpful to take a few minutes to embrace a renewed mindset about dreams from God's perspective. The following are a few statements of belief to read out loud, and then a prayer.

1. I believe that God is an all-powerful, ever-present Spirit in a spiritual Kingdom, who wants to speak to me.
2. I believe that God still communicates to people today through dreams, just as He did in Bible days.
3. I believe that dreams are part of a normal Christian life.

Prayer

Father, thank You that You have always wanted to communicate with me and have made it possible by allowing Jesus Christ to be the payment for my sin, removing the barrier between us. Forgive me for any skepticism or doubt I have had about Your existence or Your desire to speak to me through dreams. Forgive me for believing the lies of the enemy, which made me afraid of spiritual experiences. I receive forgiveness and invite You to reveal Yourself to me through Your Holy Spirit.

My Story—
No Time to Waste
Sleeping

I will pour out my Spirit upon all people. Your sons
and daughters will prophesy. Your old men will dream
dreams, and your young men will see visions.

Joel 2:28 NLT

Jealousy, curiosity and frustration described my emotions about
my dreamlessness. The stories my friends told me about their
exotic dreams triggered self-condemnation in me. *There must
be something wrong with me*, I thought, *or I would be dreaming, too.* Although I knew I was not a perfect specimen of a
Christian, they were not perfect, either. But God was talking
to them at night and not to me. Why not?

Growing up as an Episcopal priest's daughter exposed me
to the Bible, as well as the *Book of Common Prayer*. My dad
preached a salvation Gospel, believing the Bible was truth,
including the miracles. I was mesmerized by Bible stories of
walking on water, multiplying food and handwriting on the
wall (see Matthew 14:29; Mark 8:1–9; Daniel 5:5). But the Bible

stories about dreams were never emphasized. I cannot remember anyone around me ever talking about a dream they had at night. Dreams were not part of our family experience. It was okay to daydream, but there was no spiritual connection made between God and imaginative thoughts.

Dad had been a naval officer, then an attorney, before becoming a priest. He was brilliant, and his opinion, in his mind, carried the authority of God with it. This belief affected all areas of our lives, not just religion. He believed it was important to be well educated. One way to achieve this was to read books rather than watch television. Because of this belief, we did not have a TV. His love of books was contagious, although I never understood why we could not read and have a television as well. There was even room for it on the antique table next to the bookshelves in the family room. I was confident even Aunt Louise, the provider of the antique table, would have approved.

Among the classics, encyclopedias, novels and children's books in our home were my dad's seminary books. Curiosity drew me to books about spiritual things. These books had dull bindings, no pictures, a musty smell and small print, but they held an attraction more powerful than fancy graphics to grab the attention of a ten-year-old.

One reason for my gravitation to these religious textbooks was my encounter with the Holy Spirit when I was eight. My dad was diagnosed with cancer of the vocal cords. Even though I did not understand the medical ramifications of the "C" word, I was scared. We had moved to another city for Dad's radiation treatment. My parents had found a small Episcopal church near the hospital complex. At noon on Wednesdays, the church was open for a healing service. Going to a church service in the middle of the week, at lunchtime, was not something I would have chosen to do. My parents did not give me a choice.

Dad said, "You're going!"

"Yes, sir."

When I woke up Wednesday morning, I was hopeful my parents had changed their minds, but they had not. I pouted all the way to the church. When we arrived at the front of the ivy-covered church and walked through the double red doors, I felt I had entered a storybook sanctuary of peace. The refracted noon sunlight pouring through the stained glass windows added to the beauty of the old mahogany pews and blue velvet cushions. Flickering candles on the altar filled the air with a pleasant scent. I did not tell my parents, but I was glad I had come.

At a certain point in the service, I heard the priest give an invitation: "If you would like prayer for healing, come up to the altar rail."

I followed my parents to the front and knelt down on the thick, faded embroidered cushions. Out of the corner of my eye, I watched the priest move from person to person, leaning over each one, whispering something in his or her ear. He then put his hands on each one's head. I saw his lips moving but could not hear the words.

Soon he was standing in front of me, whispering in my ear, "What do you want God to do for you?"

Without even thinking, I blurted out, "I want my dad to be healed."

He gently placed both of his large hands on the top of my head and quietly prayed, "Heavenly Father, please heal this child's father. In Jesus' name, Amen."

It was such a quick, simple prayer from a stranger in an unfamiliar church, but I knew something wonderful, yet indescribable had taken place inside. My parents did not know that anything had happened to me, but I would not have been able to explain, even if they had asked. The immediate benefit to me was no more fear. Although no one discussed death around me, it was in the air. No child wants her parent to suffer or die, even if she does not like the "rules of the house." Looking back, I see that event as the start of my journey of discovery into God, a journey driven by an insatiable hunger for more.

Instinctively I connected the experience at the altar with the musty books in my dad's office. My parents did not realize they had a book thief in the house. Home alone with a babysitter, I would sneak into the office, find a book and take it to my bedroom. Nighttime for me was not scary at all. It was my favorite time. In secret, under the covers with a large flashlight, I went on a treasure hunt in the book. There was always a race to find the treasure before sleep captured me.

Fighting Sleep

Sleep was never my friend. Pregnancy must have been a challenge to my mother if I was as sleep-averse in the womb as I was as a toddler. My mother was forty when I was born. She needed naps. According to her, I was always a "handful." It was not clear to me what that meant. It did not sound good, so I never asked for details. From my perspective, it was a challenge having a mother who insisted on naps. Every day! I would play with my food at lunch as long as possible, knowing that soon I would hear the hated words: "Time for a nap."

I would argue back, "But I'm not tired!"

Her quick response was, "You need one so you won't be tired."

Occasionally there was a reprieve from the dreaded walk upstairs to the nap prison. Mother was my jailer, the baseball announcer on the radio was my uninvited companion, and loud, intermittent snoring trumpeting from Mother was my torture for several hours.

Mother, like most new mothers, felt the need to read child-rearing books to learn how not to damage this helpless, crying, eating, pooping bundle of joy. Unfortunately for me, she seemed to have learned just one principle from those books. It was the answer for every situation. I am sure there must have been other solutions, but perhaps she never finished reading the books. Yes, the answer had to do with sleep. If at any time I was not a happy, compliant, polite child, I heard these words: "You need a nap!" Imagine how many times I heard those words if I was a handful. It was one thing to have to go to bed when it was dark, but to have to go to bed in the middle of the day was outrageous. My punishment for unacceptable behavior was always either a nap or the early-to-bed sentence. Both were horrific.

As a child, for me bedtime was a cruel robber. All the fun stopped with my parents' words "Time for bed." Summertime kickball games abruptly ended at the defining moment of determining the winning team. An imaginary journey among the stars as I lay outside on the bow of our boat was terminated by those hated words. The first winning hand of Hearts, unfinished—robbed again. When I was twelve, Dad finally purchased a TV. Watching it was by permission only, however. Unless the evening TV show was deemed "important," I was banished to my bedroom. I concluded that all the fun stopped when I had to turn off the light and go to sleep.

By the time I was in college, I had been trained to see sleep as a robber who came in the form of punishment, misery and an unwelcome wet blanket on life's excitement and fun. As an undisciplined student, I saw nighttime as my savior, bailing me out, giving me the necessary extra time to write term papers, cram for exams and memorize Greek vocabulary for the Friday morning quiz. To work at night was easier. The racquetball courts, coffee shop, bookstore were all closed. The only distraction was the early morning smell of fresh bread floating up from the basement kitchen in my dorm.

After college, I lived in a house with several single women. We all had day jobs that required getting up early, making a challenge of sharing the bathroom with four others, packing lunches, grabbing breakfast and having some semblance of a quiet time. We were a mix of night owls and early morning risers. One of the girls was neither. She needed lots of sleep. I did not understand how any adult would require as much sleep as she did.

My judgment of her was internal, not vocal. Occasionally the arrogance popped out in my tone of voice. I was in charge of the house. Saturday morning was chore time. We would all drag ourselves into the kitchen, coffee in hand, to plan our work. Invariably, one of the girls was missing. Even though I knew the answer, I would still ask, "Where is Joelle?"

The answer was always the same: "She's sleeping."

For her it was not laziness or being a baby; it was physical. Without nine-plus hours of sleep, she would get severe migraines. Even with this knowledge, I wanted to bang on her door and say, "Get up. It's time to grow up!"

My pride about not needing to sleep increased, taking on a spiritual tone. Periodically, our church scheduled several days of round-the-clock prayer and fasting. Wanting to be more like Jesus, who went to the mountains at night to pray, I would always take the middle-of-the-night sessions. My night-owl life had now been sanctified. Paul wrote in Romans that I was predestined to be conformed to the image of Jesus Christ (see Romans 8:29). I concluded short nights were a prescribed part of the conforming process.

During this time in my life, I would get up at 4:00 in the morning to be at the gym to play racquetball at 4:45, having gone to bed at 1:00 a.m. or after. If it was not the gym, it was the practice range, hitting buckets of golf balls, or the track, jogging. Health and fitness were another part of holiness. My body was the temple of the Holy Spirit and needed exercise. Between late-night prayer and early morning exercise, sleep was set aside for the more important activities of a Christian life.

As a Christian, I learned the importance of serving, laying my life down. My job in a church and Christian school provided more and more opportunities to do both. Keeping a list of all the tasks was essential. It seemed there were always more things to do on the list than there were hours in the normal workday. My boss sent me to a time management conference. My takeaway was the need to prepare a prioritized to-do list the night before, in order to be effective the next day. I felt I now had permission to use the nighttime to add to, edit, rewrite and prioritize the growing notebook of responsibilities.

Seeing Visions

No one ever challenged me about my lack of sleep. I don't remember any teaching in our church about dreams and sleep. We were taught it was important to have goals and dreams for our life, but these dreams were not related to a God-inspired night dream. During this season, my hunger increased for more of God in my life. A friend told me about a conference at a church outside our network of churches. I was hungry enough to venture into an unfamiliar church. I was not disappointed.

The testimony of the speakers opened new possibilities of encounters with God through the Holy Spirit. During one of the worship sets, with my eyes closed, immersed in the sounds, I "saw" on the screen of my mind a huge marble staircase as wide as the platform. An inaudible voice said, *Come up.*

This was new, inviting and a bit scary. In my mind I heard questions: *Am I hallucinating? Is this just my imagination?* I was not sure.

My hunger for God always stirred curiosity. Books were my source to satisfy the questions in my mind and heart. The book table at the conference provided some answers, but many more questions. I was attracted to titles with words like *visions* and *dreams*. Through reading the books I bought at the conference, I learned that my experience of the marble staircase had been a vision. Further reading taught me that visions are the same as dreams, but are experiences we have while awake rather than asleep. (See question 31 in chapter 13 for a more detailed definition of these.) Although I could not generate a vision myself, I discovered that when I was in a time of worship, I often had visions. The visions had different meanings. Some were encouraging, others were instructive, others, a promise or a melody for a song.

Desiring Dreams

The visions became a regular part of my life. Dreams did not. My answer was always to buy another book to satisfy the hunger in my heart for more and answer the questions in my mind. My library on dreams rapidly grew. Any new tape series or dream course was added to the collection.

One of my dreaming friends said, "Buy the laminated dream cards." I bought all the cards and would be able to interpret the meaning of all the flowers, foods, body parts and other dream images—if I ever had a dream.

Another dreaming friend said, "Buy John Paul Jackson's *Moments with God Dream Journal*" (Streams Publications, 2002). I bought it immediately, as well as every other dream resource, sparing no expense. If I could start dreaming, it would be worth the money. The *Dream Journal* and voice recorder remained on the bedside table, empty. No recording of dreams of any kind.

It appeared to me that everyone was dreaming except me. I would try to act as interested and excited as my friends as they recounted their dreams. Dream sharing became a common part of any gathering. Soon I lost my capacity to rejoice in another's blessings as I continued to be the only one in the group without a dream to share. It was not possible to put a Christian spin on my attitude. It had become jealousy, not spiritual hunger. Added to that attitude was self-condemnation.

The Bible merely confirmed that dreams were part of the normal Christian life. I heard Joel 2:28 preached, quoted, sung more times than I needed. I wanted the Spirit to be poured out on me. I fit the qualifications: I was a woman, and a member of the human race. The evidence of the outpouring was prophecy, dreams and visions. I had none of the dreams going on in my life. If people like Abimelech, Nebuchadnezzar and Pilate's wife, all Gentiles, could have dreams (see Genesis 20:3; Daniel 2:1; Matthew 27:19), what was wrong with me? I must be really bad. Maybe God saw me as being the same "handful" I had been to my mother.

Self-condemnation has never been a source of empowerment in my life. There is no time that I remember feeling closer to God through a session of self-accusation. Distance, separation, isolation, hopelessness, bitterness, anger and frustration were always the result when traveling on the road labeled *Condemnation*. The faithful Holy Spirit kept the fire of hunger burning in me, a reminder to keep asking, seeking and knocking for the answer to my dreamlessness (see Matthew 7:7).

Humility is often the step before revelation. I was embarrassed living as a nondreamer among dreamers. I did not want to add their condemnation to my own self-accusatory thoughts. It was safer not to admit that I did not dream. Perhaps they would interpret my silence as humility. I portrayed myself as someone who did not want to boast about my experiences in God. The truth was, I had no dreams to share.

Hearing Truth

One day my false humility became genuine humility. I had a life-changing conversation with a close friend who was a dreamer.

She recounted a prophetic dream she had had the night before. With embarrassment I said to her, "I am ashamed to admit that I am jealous of you."

"Why are you jealous of me?" she asked.

"Because you always have incredible dreams. You have a whole shelf of dream journals filled with dreams. I have a shelf of journals with empty pages because I don't have any dreams. What's wrong with me?"

She started laughing. I was offended at first. I had just shared my heart, including all the ugliness of my jealousy, frustration and hopelessness. My confession to her contained a cry for help and a willingness to hear the truth even if it hurt, but not an invitation to be laughed at.

She realized I was upset. Looking me straight in the face, she said with measured intensity, "Faith, you don't sleep enough to dream!"

Stunned, I replied, "What do you mean?"

"I mean you need to sleep long enough to actually have time to dream."

I was astounded by her diagnosis. Revelation is usually truth we have never seen, imagined or even thought. Her words startled me. There is a relationship between dreams and how long one sleeps? What about Jesus spending the night in prayer? What about laying my life down in service? What about all the important things that can only be done while awake? Where does it say in the Bible we need a certain amount of sleep? What can be accomplished if I am asleep? I have a destiny. I have a lot of goals, but they will not be accomplished if I spend my life sleeping.

I came away from that conversation with more questions than I had before, but I now had a possible answer. Fortunately, my hunger for dreams had not been dampened by all the frustration and disappointment from the lack of dreams. Reviewing my life in the light of my friend's diagnosis indicated that my view of sleep would require major transformation. I realized my view of sleep as robber, punisher, wet blanket and deterrent to spiritual disciplines and physical exercise had worked against my deep desire to know God in every facet of His multidimensional being.

Dreaming Dreams

When you started reading this book, your main interest might have been just to get a good night's sleep, but after the first chapter your interest may have been piqued about the prospect of a supernatural dream from God. You might have been someone more like me, who wanted dreams but did not have any. No matter what your level of interest has been in dreams, I have good news! As I put into practice the things I am going to share in this book about God's plan for sleep and dreams, I began to dream and receive creative revelation and inspiration. My experience can be yours as well. There is hope both for sleep and dreams because God is the source of them both.

Before we look at some modern dreams, as well as some biblical ones, I want to tell you about one of my first dreams. It had to do with a book. Although I was asleep, in the dream I was just waking up, lying on my bed. I saw a tsunami of liquid gold coming toward me, enveloping me in this wave of watery substance. Even though I was underwater, I was breathing and could see what looked like the sandy floor of an ocean. Without any effort, I ended up on the bottom of the deep, next to an old red car in mint condition, one that we would call a classic. Since I am not a classic car fan, it did not mean anything to me.

Father God must have noticed my quizzical look and answered my question before I had a chance to verbalize it. He pointed to the car and said, *That's your book—but you will have to go deep to get it.*

37

I knew He was not referring to a literal ocean, but rather going deep into Him in order to receive the revelation to write it. Not bad for a novice dreamer!

Prayer

Father God, thank You that there is hope—both for sleep and for dreams. I am ready to receive information and revelation that will help position me to enjoy all the blessings You want to give me as I sleep. I am willing to go deeper in my knowledge of You. Thank You for the creative inspiration You want to give me, whether for a book, a song, a painting, an invention, a formula or a strategy.

God's Nighttime Activity

Behold, He who keeps Israel shall
neither slumber nor sleep.

Psalm 121:4

Although humans have an internal clock that is programmed for
sleep, God is not wired as we are. He never sleeps or even gets
drowsy. He does not nod off, falling in and out of sleep as we
share with Him the deep things of our heart. He does not need
sleep, as we do, to function. If He does not sleep, what does He
do? According to David, He watched over Israel as its protec-
tor. The writer of Exodus reported that God led the Israelites
in the wilderness as a pillar of fire at night (see Exodus 13:21).

God is not what modern psychology would diagnose as a
"workaholic" just because He never sleeps. According to Genesis 2:2, He worked six days on the creation project and rested
on the seventh, when He finished His work. He also lives outside
of time, so there is no way to measure the hours He "works."
What we do know is that whether at rest or at work, He is
purposeful and focused on His plan to see His lost children

restored to Him, and to see the influence of heaven, the realm of His domain, returned to earth.

The serpent's anger against God and jealousy toward Adam and Eve's relationship with Him ignited the moment he witnessed God sculpt Adam from the dust and breathe life into him. His revenge was to plant lies about the Father that, when believed, caused Adam and Eve to disobey, resulting in separation from the Father and banishment from the Garden. The repercussions from just one lie were deep and painful both for God and for Adam and Eve. God lost His kids, and they became orphans in a foreign and often frightening world.

Their loneliness that first night outside the Garden must have been extreme. No more intimate walk with God in the cool of the evening (see Genesis 3:8). No more direct physical contact with their Father and no means of face-to-face communication with Him like what they had enjoyed before. There were no telephone lines or satellite connections for them to use to "call home." Imagine how your young child would feel if he or she became separated from you in the middle of a bustling city in a hostile foreign country, with no phone. I cannot conceive of life without the ability to hear someone's voice, receive prayer or encouragement, share a laugh or get directions.

From the moment Eve took the first bite of the apple, God's plan of reconciliation went into action. No slimy serpent would rob Him of His children if they chose to come home. From mankind's perspective, it seemed like centuries of separation, but God is outside of time, so for Him a day is as a thousand years and a thousand years is just a day (see 2 Peter 3:8). God's clock has to do with completeness, not specific minutes, hours, weeks, months or years. In the fullness of time there would be the birth of the Reconciler, Jesus Christ (see Galatians 4:4).

In the meantime, God placed His Spirit on various men and woman who were appointed to speak on His behalf. The writer of Hebrews said, "God, who at various times and in various ways spoke in time past to the fathers by the prophets . . ." (Hebrews 1:1). Much of the Old Testament biblical record recounts words, encounters, dreams or visions delivered to men and women from God. The prophetic words spoken by those designated as prophets of God often came to them through a revelation in their sleep. The Old Testament makes it clear these night visions are the language of God. God's first language is dreams and visions, not English, French or Japanese.

God's desire for close fellowship through communication is not limited to a chosen few. He offers an open invitation to anyone who wants a relationship with Him. He knew Adam originated from dust and would need wisdom and guidance if he and Eve were going to survive and flourish. As a loving parent, God's attention is focused on His children, whether they are in disobedience and unbelief or are one of the returning prodigals. Rebellion never caused God to close His heart; He could not because to do so would deny His nature of love.

Starting with Abimelech's dream in Genesis 20:3, biblical writers continued to chronicle the communication from God to men and women through the ages. Sometimes these nighttime experiences were referred to as a vision of the night (see 1 Samuel 3:15; Job 20:8; Isaiah 29:7; Daniel 2:19; 7:2). Zechariah referred to his dream/vision by saying, "In a vision during the night, I saw . . ." (Zechariah 1:8 NLT). The word used to describe the event is not as important as the encounter itself, which was always marked by "seeing" and followed either by "hearing" or perceiving an explanation of what was seen. In the next chapter, we will look at five specific dreams recorded in the Bible that have had an impact on the world to the present day.

The purpose of God's interaction with His children at night, during their sleep, is to prepare them for the day. They are on a holy mission as His ambassadors to issue an invitation to all the lost children, the prodigal orphans on the earth, to come home and enjoy the goodness of the Father's love that they demonstrate as His emissaries and citizens of another country— heaven (see 2 Corinthians 5:20). The dreams He sends might give direction, strategy, wisdom, deliverance, revelation, inventive ideas or encouragement. They all originate from a Father who delights in His kids and wants to partner with them in this grand undertaking to bring the atmosphere of heaven to earth. No good father would think of sending his children on an assignment alone or without provision to accomplish the task. We may not have had a good earthly father, but we have a good heavenly Father.

The psalmist said God has given the earth to man (see Psalm 115:16). It would be cruel for God to give us a responsibility, hold us accountable for our performance and yet withhold the tools and knowledge necessary for us to do our job. The life He envisioned for us was to be in relationship with Him. Even Jesus needed the presence of His Father and the Holy Spirit to fulfill His work on earth. He said, "The Father has not left Me alone" (John 8:29). Jesus is our model for every aspect of life.

God is not interested in keeping the mysteries of the universe a secret. Paul wrote that we are "stewards of the mysteries" (1 Corinthians 4:1). Stewards in biblical days had vast responsibility. Eleazar, Abraham's servant, is an example of someone fulfilling that role (see Genesis 24:2). He was responsible for every aspect of Abraham's household. His duties included care of the house, land, crops, animals, finances, children (their health and education). To be hired for such a job, Eleazar needed to know how everything worked and be able to fix things that were not functioning properly. If the corn crop died, "I don't know" would not have been an acceptable answer to an inquiry as to why the crop failed.

We are the "Eleazars" of today, and the earth is our responsibility. God instructed Adam and Eve to take care of the Garden of Eden. That assignment has never changed. Just as God walked with Adam in the Garden in the cool of the evening, probably giving him instructions and wisdom about how to take care of the plants and animals, He wants to help us with our assignment. We are not to live as orphans. Whatever "garden" we are working in—education, government, the arts, medicine—God desires to collaborate with us. And one of the ways He does that (which many have neglected to notice) is through the instruction He gives us in dreams.

Warning Dreams

A friend of mine who lives in the New York City area told me a dream she had in 1998. Here is the dream in her own words:

> I dreamt that I was in the downtown area of Manhattan Island, behind Trinity Church. I was walking along the street called Trinity Place. Having worked downtown for many years, I was familiar with the area, but not the specific buildings on that block. I entered a gray building about twelve floors high, with two revolving doors in the lobby. While standing in the lobby with my hands and arms pressing toward the floor, I screamed, "It's safe, it's safe, it's safe!" Large numbers of people were scrambling outside in the streets and inside the building. As I said those words, I saw a great wave like a tsunami coming down the street, but nothing entered the building. Then I woke up.
>
> I shared this dream at a weekly prayer meeting at our church. My friend Ada, a school principal, told me that I described "to a T" her high school. She asked if I would come to the school one day to pray. She prayed frequently for her school, putting Scripture verses in her shoes as she walked the halls while "standing" on the promises of God. We set a day during

the summer for me to come. When I arrived at the school, I knew right away that it was the same building I had seen in the dream. We prayed as we walked through the entire school building, starting with the lobby and going floor by floor, declaring, "It's safe, it's safe!" We anointed all the elevators, doorways and stairwells with oil, and we prayed God's protection over the school.

Because Ada felt my dream was from God, she continued for the next three years to declare, "It's safe, it's safe!" as she prayed for the school building and students. She always told her students that no matter what might be going on at home, in their neighborhoods or on the subway, they would always be safe at the school. Neither of us had any idea what else the dream meant until September 11, 2001.

When I saw the news as the Twin Towers fell, and I watched the people running with that cloud of smoke behind them, I dropped to my knees at home, saying, "This is the dream!" Immediately I thought of Ada and the high school students. Her school building was located between the American Stock Exchange and another high school. On the morning of 9/11, both buildings on the right and left of Ada's school suffered structural damage; Ada's building, however, stayed structurally sound. Not one window was damaged. All her students, as well as the faculty, escaped the building, running through the streets to Battery Park at the tip of Manhattan Island.

Ada told me later that as she was evacuating the school, heading toward Battery Park, she heard a *snap*, *crackle* and *pop*. She turned around and saw a tsunami-sized wave of blackness coming toward them. At that moment she remembered my dream and knew they would be safe.

One of the teachers went back into the building to check that everyone had evacuated. Days later, he mentioned to Ada that while he was in the building, darkness came over the entire lobby. He tried to escape through the revolving door, but the door would not budge. Although the force of the cloud of debris was so intense that it would not allow the door to move, the smoke and the debris never entered the lobby!

Because Ada's school building was undamaged, and because of its proximity to Ground Zero, the building was used as a temporary morgue for many of the victims. Not a pleasant thought, but a testimony to the power of a dream, stewarded by two ordinary women who understood that as daughters of God they had responsibility and authority to bring peace and establish security on earth.

Could God have saved the children in the school without the three years of prayer? Of course! But He has chosen to invite us to work together with Him. We become His hands and His voice all over the world as we receive downloads from Him as we sleep. They may come as a dream or a revelation from His Spirit to ours, giving us knowledge of His ways, His loving thoughts about us, solutions to problems or insight about our calling. Just because we don't have dramatic experiences like this one, or even simple dreams we remember, does not mean God is not instructing us, preparing us and providing for us as we sleep.

Wooing Dreams

Just as a natural father interacts with his children in different ways, depending on the child's need, God's communication with us at night as we sleep has different content, but the same tone. All His interactions, whether through warnings for our protection or wooing through revelations, come wrapped in love. That tone of gentle love from the Father, reaching into the heart of the sleeper, is demonstrated in the recent stories of Muslims having encounters with "the Man in white" as they are sound asleep in their beds. In his book *Dreams and Visions: Is*

Jesus Awakening the Muslim World? Tom Doyle recounts story after story of dream encounters between Jesus and Muslims.

One of those stories Doyle recounts is about a Muslim woman named Aisha. Jesus appeared to her one night in her sleep, and although terrified at first, she immediately felt love flowing from Him to her. She said it was as if His eyes were speaking to her, saying, *Come with Me.* To her, this visitation was even more astounding because it took place in Mecca, the seat of Islam, during the Hajj, an annual Islamic pilgrimage—not a likely place in her mind to have such an experience with Jesus Christ. She continued to have these visions at night, each time feeling the invitation of His love to come with Him. Her cousin Reem, who lived in a different city, was having the same spiritual encounters. Jesus' pursuit of them was successful, so much so that they became a team of Bible couriers. Reem, a seamstress, would sew tiny New Testaments into the hem of Aisha's hijab, her traditional head covering, enabling her to transport them from Reem's home in Jordan back to her home in Mecca.[1]

Revelatory Dreams

Not all God's nighttime activity is mission minded. Sometimes He may simply respond to the need of one of His children, nothing world-changing, but important to Him because it is important to His child. Sarah Breedlove, born in 1867 as the daughter of two former slaves, was orphaned at age seven. Her life was difficult as a child, and becoming an adult did not change that fact. She married at fourteen and gave birth to a daughter, but found herself as a single mom after her first husband died and her second husband was unreliable. To support herself and her daughter, she cooked and did laundry, earning $1.50 a day. Besides these financial hardships, she suffered the embarrassment of going bald. Hair loss is never desirable, particularly if you are a thirty-something woman.

Sarah was a churchgoing woman, and I would imagine at some point she probably asked God to do something about her hair problem. She might even have reminded Him that since He counted the hairs on her head, He must be aware their numbers were decreasing every day (see Luke 12:7). As a good Father, He cared not only about the state of her soul, but also the condition of her scalp. He gave her a dream that ultimately led to more than a full head of hair.

In the dream, a black man came to her and told her specific ingredients to mix together and apply to her scalp. How good of God to send a black man, not a white man, to her. He was sensitive to the times, aware that in that day Sarah might not have felt safe encountering a white man while she slept, even if only in a dream. She must have felt the importance of the revelation she received, because even though some of the ingredients came from Africa, she found a way to order them. She mixed the prescribed items together, applied the concoction to her head, and after she had used it for just a few weeks, her hair grew in faster than it fell out. She assumed other balding people would be thrilled to have access to this miracle-working product. With only an initial investment of $1.25, she began to market "Madam Walker's Wonderful Hair Grower." This invention, inspired by God, resulted in Sarah's financial success as one of the first black women millionairesses in the United States, all because God had compassion on His daughter, Sarah.[2]

The three examples we have looked at reveal different types of dreams—warning, wooing and revelatory. They reveal the various ways God uses these spiritual experiences to provide for the needs of men and women, even as their bodies are being restored through sleep. We also encounter God's heart of love that cares deeply for all kinds of people—innocent children in a school; those who have rejected Him by choosing another religion; widows and orphans suffering physical hardship. Although His love cannot be measured, it can be experienced on a personal level. He is impartial; the same yesterday, today and forever; always reaching out through love for reconnection with those He created to be part of His family; working on our behalf day and night.

Prayer

Father, thank You for Your awareness of something as insignificant as the number of hairs on my head, in the midst of all the important issues that must be on Your mind. Thank You that Your activity at night is as a loving Father, watching over me as Your child, giving comfort, encouragement, wisdom and guidance to keep me safe while I sleep, as well as when I wake up. I welcome Your presence while I sleep tonight. I trust You to know what I need even before I ask, and I trust that You will supply everything I need for today.

Five Historic Encounters with God at Night

You have visited me in the night.

Psalm 17:3

As we saw in the previous chapter, our heavenly Father continues to speak today to His children through dreams. He is the God who never changes. The reason believers throughout history have made the Bible a bestseller is because reading it has never gone out of style. By acquainting ourselves with the God of Abraham, Isaac and Jacob, we have a better idea whom we are encountering in our life today. Not only is His character unchanging, but His acts are eternal, affecting generation after generation. In this chapter we will look at five different people whose night encounters with God changed not only their lives, but ours as well. I can rejoice in their experiences because I receive benefit from them even though they occurred thousands of years ago.

God's covenant-making night with Abraham and His invitation to Jacob to come up to the heavenly realm, using the same ladder as the angels, are historic events that affect my life as well. As a believer, I enjoy the unbreakable covenant relationship with God and His promises established with Abraham. The ladder giving access to the heavenly realm still stands. God's promises are not just for one, or for a select few, but for all. Both the wisdom of Solomon and many of the songs of David are the result of a historic sleep. These continue to bless me as I read Proverbs and Psalms, one the writing of Solomon, and the other primarily the writing of David. Adam was the first person who had one of these supernatural, life-altering nights. I imagine he was thankful for a good night's sleep, but even more for the unveiling of his new wife, Eve.

Creation of Eve

Once God had created Adam from the dust and brought him to life through the first mouth-to-mouth resuscitation, Adam's first task while overseeing the Garden was to name all the animals (see Genesis 2:19). Not only was this an enormous job, but also a lonely one. God recognized that Adam needed a companion other than one of the animals. Regardless of how stunning the lioness in the Garden may have been, Adam was not able to relate to her as a peer. Perhaps he befriended one of the dogs in the Garden and derived some comfort, but nothing like what he was about to experience. There are so many things left out of the Bible that would be so interesting to know! One day, when I move to heaven, I will ask Adam to tell me what went on in the Garden. For now, I can only imagine.

What did Adam and God discuss during their evening walk in the Garden? I wonder if Adam asked God what inspired Him to create some of the strange-looking animals like the hippopotamus and the giraffe. They might even have shared a laugh. Did Adam tell God he was lonely? In the absence of electricity or fire, as dusk became darkness Adam had to lie down and sleep without the comfort of another human being.

God executed a plan one night that would change Adam's single life. Once Adam was asleep, God reached into his body, removed a rib and fashioned Eve. This was the first surgery performed on earth, this time by the Great Physician Himself. Though without the aid of anesthesia or a sterile environment, the operation was a success as both Adam and Eve survived. The writer of Genesis gives no description of their first meeting other than, "He brought her to the man" (Genesis 2:22).

Adam's first response was to continue his naming assignment. When he saw Eve, he proceeded to name this new creature "woman." I am sure he had no idea how different his life would be as a result of that first introduction in the Garden. With this one encounter between Himself and Adam while Adam slept, God established the foundation of society—family.

Covenant with Abraham

The result of Abraham's nighttime visitation by God not only impacted his life, but the life of every child of God for eternity. When Abraham (then called Abram) was 75, God promised to bless him, make him famous and establish him as a great nation (see Genesis 12:1–3). He would have so many offspring that to count them would be as impossible as numbering the specks of dust on the earth (see Genesis 13:16). Anyone would be ecstatic to receive such promises. There was one problem: Sarah, Abraham's wife, had not been able to get pregnant, and her internal clock had stopped ticking.

Some years later, God appeared to Abraham again. This time He gave him an astronomy quiz to see if he knew how many stars were in the sky. Even with no city lights to dim the bright stars, it was impossible to give a precise count of twinkling stars above his head. Once again, Abraham heard God tell him he would have as many offspring as there were stars in the sky. After so many years without even one child, Abraham could not help letting God know how he felt. He trusted Him, but said he needed some assurance about these grand promises.

Because Abraham spoke with respect and not anger, God responded to him immediately with specific instructions to get a heifer, goat, ram, turtledove and pigeon. Abraham had become a wealthy man, so would have had no trouble producing these animals. The Bible does not explain why God requested this menagerie, but I imagine Abraham knew immediately that these were animals used when two individuals came into a contractual agreement, a binding covenant of promise to fulfill the terms of the contract. God wanted to assure Abraham that He would confirm all the previous promises with a blood covenant (see Genesis 15:8–18). This was not a usual occurrence, as covenants were often cut between two equals. But in this case, God was binding Himself to a human being. Only once before had God stooped to make a covenant with man. That one was with Noah after the flood. The rainbow is still the sign of God's unbroken promise never to wipe out completely the inhabitants of earth with a flood (see Genesis 9:13).

For this covenant, Abraham provided the animals and prepared them in the prescribed manner. He cut each in half and placed the halves on the ground, with one half of each animal on one side of a narrow pathway and the other half on the other side of the walkway. The traditional covenant required each of the two people making the covenant to walk between the carcasses of the dead animals to affirm the terms of the agreement, as well as the punishment of death, represented by the dead animals, in the event either party broke the contract.

Before Abraham had a chance to walk the walk of covenant through the dead animal path, he fell asleep. This would not seem like the best time to nod off! But it was all part of the plan. God took the covenant-cutting walk by Himself, to indicate that the burden of the fulfillment of the promise was His alone. Abraham was to be the recipient of all the promises. The power of covenant is both the fact that it is unbreakable and also that it is eternal. That one event thousands of years ago meant God bound Himself to make Abraham and all his descendants, including those of us today who are related to Abraham through faith in Jesus Christ, to be blessed and to bless others (see Galatians 3:9, 29).

Open Heaven

Jacob, Abraham's grandson, had an encounter with God in a dream that revealed a truth about heaven that we can enjoy today. The setting for this encounter would be called Bethel. Jacob was on his way to Harran, home of Laban, his uncle, where he had fled at his mother's suggestion to escape the wrath of his furious brother, Esau, whom he had cheated out of his inheritance. Harran might offer family connections, but not great physical comforts. It was located in what is today southeastern Turkey, and the name itself came from an Arabic word meaning "hot." One traveler in the area described it this way: "Stripped from the grassy lands and shades, it seems like Harran's name comes from its own climate. Every part of it is boiling hot. You can neither find shade, nor breathe normally."[1]

The journey from Beersheba to Bethel was about 78 miles, about an hour in a car or several days on foot. From Bethel, Jacob would have another 400-plus miles to his destination. This was not a joyous trip. He had left his home, as well as his aged, blind father, Isaac; his mother, Rebekah, who had aided him in his deceit; and his enraged brother. His only companion and comforter was God. His departure was sudden, his provisions minimal. A rock was his pillow, the desert sand his mattress. If he had worn a sleep-tracking watch, it probably would have shown many restless movements during the night.

Sometime during the night, Jacob had a dream. God knew he needed encouragement, and he received it that night. Even though Jacob had deceived his father and robbed his brother, God did not abandon him. He could not, because of the covenant made with Jacob's grandfather, Abraham. We may forget about a covenant or even break it. God does not. He cannot, because that would go against His nature.

Jacob saw a ladder rising from the ground into heaven. The angels went up and down this stairway. God stood at the top of it, repeating the same promises He had made to Abraham. He had told Abraham He would be his shield. To Jacob He promised protection and companionship (see Genesis 28:13–15). The response from Jacob was worship. The God of his grandfather and father became his God. He had known about Him as a child, but now he knew Him personally. He named the location *Bethel*, meaning "house of God." This access into God's own house was not just for Jacob, but also for all the children of Abraham related through faith in Jesus Christ. We, too, are welcome to go through Jesus, the door, up the stairs to our Father's house. That might have been the best night's sleep Jacob had ever had, even though his pillow was a rock.

Wealth and Wisdom

King Solomon's encounter at night grabs my attention because it happened through a conversation he had with God in a dream (see 1 Kings 3:5). Even if he could have had an iPhone to make a voice note in the middle of the night to document the dialogue, I doubt he would have needed to. Imagine God coming to you in a dream, giving you permission to "ask for whatever you want me to give you" (1 Kings 3:5 NIV). What would your answer be? Do you think you would ever forget it? I know I wouldn't! I don't believe King Solomon did, either. The results of this one night determined his place in history forever.

Solomon asked for an "understanding heart" (1 Kings 3:9). God's response to his request was to give him wisdom more than anyone had ever had, or ever would have, and in addition, extreme wealth. His name became synonymous with great sagacity. To be told you have the "wisdom of Solomon" is a high compliment. His wealth was so excessive that the Queen of Sheba travelled approximately fifteen hundred miles by camel to witness it herself.[2] When she took a tour of his palace, even his table settings stunned her (see 1 Kings 10:4–5). I wonder if she needed smelling salts once she was taken to the vaults that housed his gold and silver.

I don't believe that on the night of his encounter with God, Solomon went to bed thinking, *Tonight is my lucky night*. His parents had trained him to set his internal compass on God—the true North. In Solomon's advice to his own son, Proverbs recounts much of what he was taught as a child. It is evident that he heard what his parents told him, because it stayed with him, guided him and became the foundation of his own parenting. He learned to be tuned in to God even in his sleep, and that skill paid great dividends to him and all future generations who have benefited from his wisdom.

Songs Downloaded

Centuries before the iCloud, there was the God Cloud. It is common today for us to receive songs downloaded from the invisible iCloud somewhere in space. But the reason we have tunes on iTunes is that God sang and shared His breath so people could sing. The man whose name will be number one for all time on the Top 100 list of songs will be King David. His Gospel choir, dressed in Levitical robes and singing, dancing, clapping and shouting to the sounds of trumpets, cymbals, tambourines and drums, will be the most-watched music video. We may have more "techlicious" instruments today, but his band had more presence. He is the father of every band that has ever led a group of believers into the courts of heaven.

King David did not start as a rock star, but as a shepherd boy who laid his head on a rock under the stars and plunked his harp, getting callouses finding new chords. Shepherding is a lonely occupation; just you and the sheep with warm coats but limited vocabulary. It is *bah-bah* this and *bah-bah* that every day. He grew up with stories of angels of the Lord, and of God Himself talking with men. In his solitude, singing to himself, he did not realize God was listening. Yet God's ears are always tuned to His children.

The writer of Job reported that God "gives songs in the night" (Job 35:10). The word for *song* here is the same word that means psalm. It is evident in some of the psalms that David or another writer was aware of a specific verse in Job and was quoting it. (Compare Job 7:17 to Psalm 8:4, and Job 5:17 to Psalm 94:12.) When David wrote in Psalm 42:8 (NET) that "by night he [God] gives me a song," however, I believe it came from his personal experience, not from a quote out of Job. The Hebrew word for *song* in this verse means "lyric song," "religious song" or "song of Levitical choirs."[3] David is not credited with writing all 150 psalms, yet he is seen as the one who established a revolutionary form of 24/7 worship emulated today by Christians around the world who host 24-hour worship conferences. Only God and David know which of his songs were ones he received in a dream from God while he slept with his sheep under the stars, but all his music released the atmosphere of heaven, calming even King Saul's psychotic rages (see 1 Samuel

16:23). His musical legacy carried on to his son Solomon, who wrote 1,005 songs, although he is better known for his wisdom than his songs (see 1 Kings 4:32).

Tonight's Encounters

As we saw in chapter 3, these nighttime encounters did not end in Bible days. God is still eager to do His mysterious, miraculous, mind-boggling nighttime escapades on our behalf through dreams, revelations and songs.

God still downloads strategies, wisdom, comfort, deliverance, solutions to problems and warnings in the night. Tonight you could encounter any of these in your dreams. There are still new ideas to birth from heaven—blueprints for governments, choreography from dances around the throne, new sounds from instruments to be invented. The list goes on and on and on.

God is never at a loss for ideas and is always awake, ready to respond as we turn our hearts toward Him and drift off into the safety of His pavilion of darkness, from which He downloads treasures (see Isaiah 45:3). As I learned from my friend, the key to having these experiences with God is for me to sleep. In the next two chapters, we will explore the gift of sleep.

Prayer

Father, thank You that I benefit today from Your gifts that You gave to men and women as they slept centuries ago. I am grateful for the possibility of family, covenant with You, access to heaven, wisdom and the gift of songs. It is comforting to know that You are willing to share the treasures of the darkness with me, as much as You did with Adam and Eve, Abraham, Jacob, Solomon and David.

5

My Body Was Designed for Sleep

I will praise You, for I am fearfully and wonderfully made.

Psalm 139:14

Although I realized sleep was a prerequisite for a dream life, I still was not convinced it was not a waste of precious time that I could use to do a lot of fun, interesting or productive things. But by the end of my study on sleep, two things happened: (1) I was convicted that I had robbed my body of sleep; (2) I was convinced that I needed to invest more time in sleep, not just for the sake of dreams, but for the well-being of my body, mind and emotions.

I encourage you to stay with me through this chapter, although I may delve into some of the scientific/medical aspects of sleep, because I believe the information is helpful in taking back our night. For me to give up my short nights, I had to be convinced of the "why" of making such a radical change in my lifestyle. I have scientific studies to thank for giving me concrete reasons to alter my thinking. On the other hand, if you are someone who wants to sleep and is unable to enjoy undisturbed sleep, this chapter should encourage you to believe that if God designed our bodies with sleep as a necessity for top performance, then He will help restore good sleep to you. Furthermore, as you read about some of the benefits of sleep and begin to feel a bit of anxiety for having been robbed of sleep, don't go to fear. Remember, the God who created your body can also heal and restore it. There is hope!

Sleep Mechanics

From the 1930s onward, because of advances in science we have learned a great deal about the benefits of sleep. By using an EEG (electroencephalogram), scientists can record the brain waves or activity in the brain. These scientific findings give us insight into our divine design and the benefits God instituted for us while we sleep. Now it is possible to go to a sleep clinic so that our brain activity can be observed during sleep or the time during the night when our sleep is disturbed.

For the purpose of discussion, it is helpful to understand a bit about the mechanics of our sleep. The former president of the American Academy of Sleep Medicine, Lawrence Epstein, and his colleague, Steve Mardon, noted that sleep can be divided into two categories: non-REM sleep and rapid eye movement (REM) sleep.[1] We spend varied amounts of time in each category of sleep, and we cycle in and out of these stages throughout the entire night.

The non-REM sleep category includes four stages. This type of sleep is the time we begin to drift off or doze. With our eyes closed, sensory input is reduced, but we can easily be aroused and awakened from this state. We typically move into stage 1 sleep, which occurs when our brain begins to slow down and we are no longer attuned to our environment. We then fall into stage 2 sleep. Here, our eyes are not moving, our heart rate has lowered, but we can still be easily startled by noise during this time of sleep. You may relate to non-REM sleep if you have children and have ever been wakened numerous times during the night by a crying baby who wants to be fed again. There is not a lot of sleep for parents during that stage of parenting, but the season will change and rest will return.

When we reach stages 3 and 4, we enter what is referred to as deep sleep. During these stages, our blood pressure drops even lower than in previous stages, and we become harder to rouse from our slumber. We experience deep sleep during earlier periods of the night. This is the time when our body experiences a number of restorative benefits, including a bolstering of our immune system, and muscle growth and repair. If you are being robbed of stage 3 and 4 sleep, remember, God can restore to you anything you did not receive due to lack of sleep. That statement is not a license to continue being a night owl on purpose, as I was. It is merely affirming the goodness of God to take care of His children.

Recent research also suggests that our memories from the day are affected during the stages of deep sleep.[2] While there is still a lot of learning taking place on the subject of sleep and memory, the general idea is that our memories are strengthened or set while we sleep. For example, when people go without sleep, they may not be able to remember tasks they just learned as well as when they have experienced sufficient sleep. It seems that sleep helps a person solidify what he or she may have learned during the day.[3] In other words, make sure to sleep before an exam!

REM Sleep

The second category of sleep is called REM sleep, or rapid eye movement sleep. This type of sleep is called REM because the eyes, although closed, are known to move during it. REM sleep is known as the time in which we dream. During REM sleep, the brain and other systems in our body are more active. REM sleep is thought to replenish our minds, while enhancing what we have recently learned. Recent research has examined the effects of REM sleep on memory. Specifically, it is thought to be an important type of sleep for preparing our memories and putting them into long-term memory (i.e., the things that you remember over time, not just your last meal).[4]

Depending on our age and barring other sleep issues, the average person may experience three to five cycles of REM sleep a night, with longer periods toward the waking hours. In other words, we usually experience longer periods of dreaming closer to the time we wake up from a full night of sleep. Although dreaming can take place in both categories of sleep (non-REM and REM sleep), it is currently thought that the quality of dreams during REM sleep is different from that of dreams during non-REM sleep. That is, REM dreams tend to be longer and have the characteristics of being more detailed and vivid.[5]

So yes, everyone dreams![6] The issue is whether we remember the dreams. From a scientific standpoint, remembrance is likely related to when we wake up and if it is during or soon after a dream. The important point here is that science has confirmed what the Bible says—that there is a lot of activity going on while we sleep. The divine design is interaction between our body, mind and emotions with the Holy Spirit. Remember Solomon? He said, "I sleep, but my heart is awake" (Song of Solomon 5:2).

Sleep Benefits for the Body

Sleep is so important to our health and mental well-being that when there is a deficit, our bodies will bypass the first several stages and head directly into stages where restoration occurs.[7] It seems we were wired for sleep. Without it, our immune system is compromised.[8] Sleep helps us fight infectious diseases and other debilitating illnesses. For example, sleep lowers the risk for cardiovascular disease, obesity and diabetes.

What follows is a list of known complications, as well as benefits, that may occur depending on proper sleep, or lack of it. While I did not use this list on myself as a diagnostic tool, it helped bring awareness to a much-needed, but too often deprived area in my life—rest and sleep. The list is also intended as a tool to facilitate an initial conversation with your heavenly Father about your physical, emotional and spiritual well-being as it relates to sleep. For some people, it may involve receiving hope for a return of sleep and health; for others like me, it may mean receiving forgiveness for robbing our body of rest.

1. Increased sleep duration and quality may increase life span.

Substantial scientific evidence suggests that there is a relationship between sleep duration and the risk of mortality.[9] Although there are some disputes to this claim that sleep patterns affect life span, there is also much scientific evidence that supports it.[10] Some caveats may be that our sleep patterns tend to change with age. This information was a good reason for me to get more sleep. I could continue with short nights and perhaps a shorter life, or longer nights and a longer life in which to do all the things I wanted to do. It made sense for me to go for the longer nights. Once again, if you are suffering with short nights, but not by choice, God is able to make up for the lost sleep and do a reset of the systems in your body. Bottom line—He appoints the number of our days as His children.

2. Proper sleep may reduce infection and inflammation in the body.

There is some evidence to suggest that inflammation in the body can lead to diseases such as diabetes, arthritic conditions and cardiovascular problems, to name a few. Scientific study reveals more every day about the wonders of our God-designed and created body. Some research findings suggest that shorter amounts of sleep may lead to inflammation in the body, which may be the primary cause of many diseases.[11] It is easy sometimes to get so caught up with life that we take for granted the vehicle of our body that enables us to live life. David got it when he praised God in Psalm 139:14 that he was "fearfully and wonderfully made."

3. Adequate sleep may reduce the risk for diabetes, obesity and heart problems.[12]

Risk for obesity is higher for both adults and children when a sleep deficit is present.[13] In a review of 45 studies, there was a 60 to 80 percent greater likelihood that an obese child or adult was also a short sleeper.[14] Also, there seems to be a relationship between sleep duration and the risk for type 2 diabetes.[15] Other studies have found that a person's sleep duration can also predict hypertension, stroke and other cardiovascular conditions.[16] Getting a good night's sleep will not cancel the effect of living a lifestyle of not exercising, or supersizing our meals. It would be nice if we could just eat what we wanted and then sleep it off.

It may seem redundant for me to emphasize once again that just because you have a sleep deficit does not mean you are going to develop diabetes or have a stroke. The goal of this book is not to scare you because of lack of sleep, but rather, to encourage you to believe that God's gift to us, and to our body, is sleep. He has a solution for anything that hinders our body from receiving what it needs through sleep, or any harm done by the lack of sleep.

4. Sleep improves athletic performance and motor skills.

One study found that participants who had not slept for seventeen to nineteen hours had motor response times equal to or lower than participants with blood alcohol levels at .05 percent (decreased inhibition, mild effects of alcohol).[17] As the lack of sleep increased, response times slowed to, or were worse than, those of participants with blood alcohol levels at .1 percent (possible slurred speech, change in motor control and reaction time caused by alcohol). This suggests that sleep is crucial for tasks or industries that involve our motor skills.

One study showed that sleep deprivation is a factor in sports-related injuries.[18] Students were injured nearly two times more when they slept fewer hours a night. In another study, college athletes reported improved motor abilities, reaction times and overall physical and mental well-being with increased sleep.[19] Thinking back to my life as a college athlete who hardly slept at all, I wonder what the outcome would have been of some of my tennis matches if I had had a good night's sleep before the competition.

5. Sleep enhances creativity, memory and learning.

As I mentioned, there are a number of scientifically documented sleep benefits that affect our mental and emotional well-being. It is thought that we experience these benefits during REM sleep or dream sleep. REM sleep helps us process and retain information, increases our problem-solving capabilities and heightens our ability to perform at work or in academics (see the earlier section on sleep mechanics). More recently, sleep theorists have suggested that sleep also plays an important role with our memory. Sleep may, in fact, help transform current information into long-term memory.[20]

When someone gets the optimal amount of sleep, it has been well documented that memory, creativity and learning are enhanced.[21] Conversely, when sleep is lacking, our capacity to learn and retain information may be impaired. In fact, without sleep we don't function at our highest thinking capacities or our best abilities to solve problems.[22] A lack of sleep is also thought to affect creativity.[23] Creativity may peak following an "incubation period," or a time away from a task. An incubation period can be necessary to enhance creative thought or action, and in this case time away is provided by sleep. Without it, our creative capacities may be stunted. We have all heard the phrase "sleep on it." Even without the benefit of recent scientific studies, people have realized that if they had a problem to solve or were stuck in a creative project, after a good night's sleep they often woke up with the solution or inspiration to move forward. This correlates with the thesis of this book, which is that God intends to download inspiration, revelation and wisdom at night, while we sleep.

6. Learning new things may require more sleep.

Some sleep theories suggest that our need for sleep might relate to the amount of new information we are learning. A decrease in the need for sleep, often observed in the elderly, may relate to the lack of stimulation in their environment.[24] Just because research shows that the older someone gets, the less sleep he or she seems to need, this does not reflect God's original design. When we read the exploits of Moses and Abraham and other patriarchs in the Old Testament, it would appear they did not slow down as they aged. In fact, Deuteronomy 34:7 states, "Moses was one hundred and twenty years old when he died. His eyes were not dim nor his natural vigor diminished." Moses did not have access to a smart watch to record his sleep, so we cannot compare his sleep patterns at the age of 100 with present-day elderly people. Yet if, as the Bible states, he was as vigorous at 120 as he was as a young man, he probably slept as much as well. Old age was never intended to be a vegetative state of inactivity of brain and body.

7. Sleep heightens academic and work performance.[25]

There seems to be a correlation between sleep deficit and lower grade point averages, and also poorer academic performance.[26] Differences in work performance were observed between workers who slept five hours or fewer and other workers. Study participants who slept fewer than five hours were at the highest risk for poor work in a manufacturing profession.[27] But citing lack of sleep to a professor or boss may not provide a valid excuse if, in fact, poor performance resulted from a lack of study or preparation instead.

8. Sleep reduces stress and bolsters emotional stability.

Recent research suggests there may be a relationship between REM sleep and the networks in our brain involved with emotions and fear (i.e., the amygdala and brain stem).[28] This suggests REM sleep may affect our emotions and memories related to fear. Of course, it makes sense that without sleep, a person may have emotional difficulties. Studies have affirmed that there is a relationship between lack of sleep or insomnia and depression,[29] along with some other mental and emotional problems, including anxiety.[30] Sometimes this becomes a catch-22 situation if a person is depressed or anxious, which causes insomnia, which then increases depression or anxiety because of the lack of sleep.

It is at this point that we may find ourselves putting blame on our body. Our body is designed to take orders from our brain, which is to be instructed by our spirit, which is to be inspired by the Holy Spirit living in us as believers. If we suffer with insomnia and don't understand God's design, it is possible to get angry with our body for not letting us sleep. It is not the body's fault, because it is simply following whatever signals are being sent from the mind or emotions. We may need to ask our body to forgive us for falsely accusing it of being the problem. In my case, I had to ask my body to forgive me for making it function without the proper sleep that God intended it to have.

Regardless of whether the emotional needs preceded the sleeplessness or not, God is the ultimate answer to the problem. The more we trust Him as a loving, compassionate God, the more we will be able to experience His help either with the anxiety or the insomnia. In chapters 7 and 9 we will look at ways to deal with anxiety and some of the other emotional issues that may contribute to insomnia.

Prayer

Father, thank You that I am fearfully and wonderfully made. You knit me together in my mother's womb. Forgive me for any time that I have not taken care of my body by not giving it enough time to rest. I receive Your forgiveness. Body, forgive me for any time I have blamed you for hindering me from sleeping. Thank You, Father, that I don't need to fear the repercussions of lack of sleep, because You are the God who heals and restores. I commit my days and nights to You, as well as my body, trusting in Your loving care.

God's Gift
of Sleep

He gives His beloved sleep.

Psalm 127:2

Everybody in every culture, from the beginning of time, sleeps. No anthropologist has ever unearthed a tribe of people who did not sleep. Sleep is as universal as breathing. This is a comforting fact, particularly if you are one who suffers from any degree of sleep disorder. There is an answer for sleep disturbance, just as there are answers for breathing problems. It is not as though you were left out when the sleep mechanism was implanted (deep sigh of relief).

As we have seen in the previous chapter, the body was designed for sleep, a necessary part of the divine plan for human beings. We are wired for it at the cellular level. David, in Psalm 127:2, described it as a gift from God to His beloved. Sometimes the immediate response we feel on a subconscious level to an endearing description from God is, *He can't be referring to me, because I'm not worthy.* The truth is that we are all

God's beloveds. The Greek word for *beloved* comes from the same word used in the well-known verse John 3:16: "God so loved the world that He gave His only begotten Son. . . ." The word *love* in this verse is derived from the Greek word *agapaō*, which means "to welcome, to entertain, to be fond of, to love dearly."[1]

God's invitation to us is as sinners, not saints. He does not reserve His love for those who have a perfect report card. Paul confirmed this by saying that "God demonstrates His own love toward us, in that while we were still sinners, Christ died for us" (Romans 5:8). You may still feel disqualified, rehearsing in your mind a lifelong list of why you are not worthy and have no hope of changing your status. Good news: Inclusion in the length, depth, breadth and height of God's love does not depend on your merit. His nature is love; love with no limits, restrictions or qualifications. He loves you because He is love, and as love He can do nothing but love. In an inexplicable way, He has bound Himself by love to act only from love. So, as ones loved by God, you and I are recipients of the gift of sleep from our Creator Father.

It is reassuring to read of people in the Bible who did not always enjoy this gift. I am not implying there is anything encouraging about insomnia. Peter told his readers in 1 Peter 5:9 to remember in their trials that their brothers and sisters all over the world were going through a similar battle against the adversary (in this case, the devil). If I know others have the same challenge as I do, it helps me believe that I am not weird, and that my situation is not uncommon. This can help me draw strength from other people's victory because my struggle is similar to theirs.

Today, if we heard a story like the one in the Bible about Job and his situation, we would all agree it was traumatic and extremely painful. He had lost his children, his health, his wealth and the support of his wife, who suggested he reject God. Her counsel was, "Curse God and die!" (Job 2:9). What a helpmeet she turned out to be in a crisis. No wonder Job suffered with sleepless nights. He describes his situation in Job 7:4–6:

> When I lie down, I say, "When shall I arise, and the night be ended?" For I have had my fill of tossing till dawn. My flesh is caked with worms and dust, my skin is cracked and breaks out afresh. My days are swifter than a weaver's shuttle, and are spent without hope.

Although we may not be able to identify with some of Job's specific symptoms, we can relate to the anguish of wondering when the night will end. The experience of lying in bed, trapped in wakefulness when others are sleeping, perhaps even next to us in bed, is miserable.

Sleep Problems and Solutions

Although you may not experience sleep deprivation, you may know someone who would give anything to have a "normal" night's sleep. The number of people in that category is astounding. There are several sleep disruptions that people report, such as nightmares, sleepwalking and night terrors. Out of all the sleep complaints people experience, insomnia is the most commonly reported problem and is reported more often among women than men.[2] In a review of 31 sleep studies, the risk for insomnia was about 1 ½ times greater for women. There may be a variety of reasons for the observed differences, but one thought is that women tend to report anxiety and depression at higher rates than men.[3]

Studies can be helpful not only to show us we are not alone, but also to give us a template for what science and medicine have determined is "good sleep." Just because you don't sleep ten hours, the way you did as a teenager, does not mean you have a sleep problem. Insomnia refers to problems people have falling asleep, staying asleep, waking up too early or experiencing a continual feeling of fatigue after several nights, weeks or even months without adequate rest.[4]

Don't worry; you don't have insomnia if you had trouble sleeping last night because you drank a mocha Frappuccino with extra whipped cream at seven in the evening. There are many ways to define quality sleep, but simply put, good sleep happens when we are able to fall asleep, stay asleep and wake up refreshed.

We Need Sleep!

Unfortunately, more and more people are reporting less than optimal sleep at night. Although science and medicine have made discoveries that extend and improve the quality of our life, no pill has been invented that enables our body to function at optimum performance with less than the normal number of hours of sleep. I don't think one ever will be invented, because just as the body cannot function without air, it cannot survive without sleep.

There is general agreement that roughly 30 percent of adults in various international studies deal with the diagnostic symptoms of insomnia.[5] Often those with depression and anxiety disorders[6] and other medical conditions[7] also suffer from insomnia, which has been on the rise over several decades in both the United States and other countries.[8, 9] The universal rise in sleep disorders is probably caused by one of these factors, or a combination of them:

- Obesity-related sleep apnea
- Increased use of social media and electronics at night

- Recession-related financial concerns
- Medical conditions
- Diabetes
- Heart disease
- Anxiety and depression
- Lifestyle of work/travel

Job's insomnia fit some of the items on the list of causes. He suffered with medical issues, financial problems and depression. He was spared the added issues of jet lag and social media overload. In his day there were not many options for dealing with sleeplessness. His first and last recourse was God.

Today, we have a medicine cabinet full of options. There are roughly twenty medications used to treat primary insomnia in adults and four to help with it.[10] You may have seen some of these medicines advertised on TV. You know, the commercials that end with a list of things that warn you about the growth of excess hair, swelling of your limbs, or that you may turn into one of the half-man, half-creatures from C. S. Lewis's *The Lion, the Witch and the Wardrobe*. According to the Centers for Disease Control and Prevention, nine million Americans are currently on prescription medication for insomnia.[11] If you are taking one of these medicines, these facts ought not make you feel guilty or ashamed. Thank God there are some options to alleviate the problem of sleeplessness. Do not stop taking any prescription sleep aids without your doctor's approval.

Besides the medications used when insomnia is a primary problem, there are also roughly 160 medications used to treat problems such as depression that are known to be associated with sleep disturbances.[12] Some people also use supplements that contain ingredients thought to lessen anxiety, insomnia and in some cases depression. Once again, if you are taking any of these drugs, please do not feel condemnation! Be thankful that science and medicine have discovered some therapies that can help you deal with this issue.

Other people use a machine that emits a pulsing blue light that guides them into a controlled breathing pattern. The purpose is to help the mind and body relax by adjusting a person's breathing pattern. Other sleep aids include CDs that are supposed to promote deep-sleep brain activity. There are also numerous types of sound machines with white noise, ocean waves and the like.

Then there are sleep masks, earplugs and dental guards for those who clench their jaw or grind their teeth. On top of all the apparatuses designed to leave us with a better night's sleep, there are many other methods such as psychological therapy, exercise, massage and meditation to help people relieve an anxious or depressed mind that is also coping with insomnia.[13] There are many other suggestions on the market for those suffering from insomnia and other sleep disturbances. You can find websites, books, online stores and products galore, all with the aim of giving you a better night of sleep. Some of these things have merit, but they lack the most important sleep aid of all—God!

Practical Solutions

In the next several chapters we will look at God's solutions for sleep issues. But first, let's examine some practical things we can do to set the stage for a good night's sleep. Here are a few suggestions made by the National Sleep Foundation. The ideal sleeping environment includes a completely dark room, with no lights from lamps or electronic devices, or light from the outside.[14] I visited a friend in New York who lived in a 450-square-foot apartment. Everything was in one room except the bathroom and tiny kitchen. My bed was a couch facing the electronic command center of her office/media center. It looked like the cockpit of an airplane—red lights, green lights blinking, white lights flashing. In addition, the noise of police sirens, trash collectors and late-night partygoers invaded the room through the windows—all robbers of sleep. Until I figured out a solution, I was sleepless in Manhattan.

A quiet environment also helps improve one's sleep. Using a white noise machine, fan, air conditioner or some type of quiet music can be conducive to good sleep. It is recommended that the room where you sleep be a peaceful and welcoming environment. This means keeping your room free from clutter, papers or anything that symbolizes work, but filling the space with colors and decorative items that symbolize comfort and rest. It also may mean buying a new bed. This seems obvious, but sometimes we endure a bad mattress because of the cost of a new one. We may decide to save money and keep the old one, but we end up spending as much or more on a chiropractor.

This next one is a hard one for me, and perhaps for you. Your sleep environment and bed should not be a place that your mind associates with work. This also means no social media in bed! It is also important to keep the sleeping environment free from electronic devices, which only serve to keep the mind active instead of promoting rest. Your bed should not be the place where you check e-mails or Facebook or post your latest thought.

Another guideline for optimal sleep has to do with temperature. Whenever possible, it is best to keep your sleeping environment cool. Our body temperature lowers when we are asleep. A room temperature between 60 and 67 degrees helps our body transition to a sleep state.[15] For those of you who wear sweaters in 100-degree weather, this may not be good news. If you are having trouble getting a good night's sleep, however, it might be good to turn the thermostat down and put on your winter pj's and thick socks. Sweet sleep is worth a cold nose.

Physical conditions can be a source of sleep disruptions. These can include sleep apnea (an obstruction in the breathing airways), physical pain, snoring, restless leg syndrome, indigestion, allergies, flu and colds, breathing conditions and taking some medications.[16] As mentioned before, people with depression and anxiety symptoms often experience insomnia. For those with anxiety, the problem may be falling asleep, and for others, the trouble may be staying asleep.

No matter what the cause of the sleep problem, whether in adults or children, there are several sleep aids that can help. Here are the ones I have found helpful.

One is to have the Scriptures playing softly all night in the bedroom. Many different translations of the Bible have been recorded, some of them dramatized with music. One such app is called Bible.is and is available at www.bible.is or on iTunes.

Another helpful aid is to have quiet, peaceful Christian music on throughout the night. Several years ago, partly for my own use, and also at the suggestion of friends, I cut an instrumental CD of my own music called "Age to Come." Using a keyboard, I played all the tracks on the CD at about fifty beats per minute—a slow, calm tempo. Later, I learned that music therapists often use music with a tempo slower than the normal human heart rate of sixty beats per minute to bring a person into a place of rest. I believe it is not only the tempo, but more importantly, the presence of God in my CDs that has the calming effect. Since the release of that first CD and those that followed, I have heard many testimonies from people who have kept my CDs playing all night and have found their sleep much improved. (See my website, www.faithblatchford.com, for more information about the instrumental CDs.)

The Giver of Sleep

Regardless of the physical problems, the good news, besides possible medications or environmental adjustments, is that God, the giver of sweet sleep, is able to heal any physical or emotional issues.

The end of Job's story is confirmation of that. Job never gave up trusting God. I bet he was glad he did not take his wife's advice. In the end the Bible says, "Now the Lord blessed the latter days of Job more than his beginning" (Job 42:12). The blessings included restoration of his health, family and wealth. Since the loss of those had contributed to his insomnia, I would imagine sleep returned to Job as well.

In the next chapters we will examine some of the emotional and spiritual inhibitors of sleep and how to deal with them.

Prayer

Father, thank You that I am Your beloved and that You bless me with the gift of sleep. My desire is to experience the fullness of that gift every night. I invite You to show me any practical thing I could do to improve my sleep at night. Jesus, thank You that Scripture says You took onto Yourself, when You hung on the cross, not only all my sins, but also all my sickness and pain, to bring healing to my body, mind and emotions. Although this is a mystery and not something I feel I deserve, I receive my healing now. Thank You in advance that my testimony will be the same as Job's. There is hope, and I choose to believe my future years will be more blessed than my past.

I've Been Robbed

The Lord said that he would dwell in the thick darkness.

1 Kings 8:12 KJV

Have you ever been robbed? If so, after the initial fear, anger may have boiled up. The conversation in your head with the robber probably went something like this: *Who do you think you are, breaking into my space and taking what belongs to me?!?* The next step after you cool down is to figure out how the felon got in and what you can do to make sure no other criminal gains access. There is a saying, "A man's home is his castle." I picture a medieval stone building, impenetrable, watchtowers on all corners, deep moat with alligators, drawbridge on pulleys, and a small peephole in the door at the end of the drawbridge, manned by a well-armed guard. Without an invitation from the master of the castle, you approach at your own risk—the risk of death.

I was robbed, but not of material goods, and not by robbers the police could capture and lock up. The thievery I am talking about takes place at night and steals my sleep and the treasures God intends to give me as I sleep. In the previous chapters, we discovered the Creator's built-in design of sleep as a means of the body restoring and refueling all its organs and systems. Historically, we have seen the activity of the God who never sleeps, busy at night bringing wisdom, strategies, creative ideas, songs, promises, encouragement to His children while they sleep, equipping them for their day's task. But from the insomnia statistics we have seen, it would appear that millions of people are being robbed of God's provision for them during sleep.

The mastermind behind some of the theft is Satan, and his gang of hoodlum demons who carry out the crime. If I was honest and we were sitting across from each other drinking coffee, I would probably say that they carry out all the theft, rather than just some of it. For now, I will leave it at some because I don't want to get into a battle of words. We have another more important battle to understand at the moment. Our battle is not against sleeplessness, even though if you are one of the seventy million people suffering with it, you probably would disagree since you feel you have been in something as fierce as hand-to-hand combat many nights, leaving the battlefield in the morning in defeat. Others may have slept, but not the sweet sleep promised in the Bible, because they wake up feeling as if an eighteen-wheeler ran over them during the night. Finally, there are those like me who, through lack of knowledge about sleep and God's intent, did not know they had been robbed by their decision to sleep as little as possible.

Points of Entry—Ignorance and Deception

Just as you would locate the entry points for a burglar in your home, I have identified two major access routes for the night hoodlums who rob us of our sleep: ignorance and deception. Although some have said ignorance is bliss, in this context it is the exact opposite. If I am ignorant about the high crime rate in my neighborhood, I may find I have been robbed if I leave my doors and windows unlocked, the keys in my ignition and my valuables spread out on the picnic table in the backyard. Knowledge of the number of robberies in my area might have motivated me to do some practical things to protect my property and possessions.

Deception and ignorance are not the same, yet they are two sides of the same coin. If I am ignorant, I do not function in the truth of the situation, which means I live in deception. But if I am deceived, it is because I am ignorant of the truth. In the context of this book, ignorance would be a lack of knowledge about God's design and intent for us as we sleep at night. Deception would include believing in lies about sleep, the night and darkness, which could hinder us from peaceful nights.

Paul declared that he was not going to be taken advantage of by Satan because he was "not ignorant of his schemes" (2 Corinthians 2:11 NASB). One of Satan's major tactics is the use of fear, which is always based on deception. Perhaps you have seen the acronym for fear: False Evidence Appearing Real. Let's look at one specific fear—fear of the dark—a little more closely.

Fear of the Dark

One of Satan's strategies to rob us of sleep at night is to create fear of the dark. Worldwide, people admit to experiencing this torment. Studies done regarding children and fear indicate more than 90 percent experience fear, the most common form being fear of the dark, which often results in poor sleep.[1] A YouGov survey of two thousand adults identified that 40 percent of them were afraid to walk around their house at night with the lights off, and one in ten would not even go to the bathroom because they were so afraid of the dark.[2] There may be a connection between fear of the dark and poor sleep at night. A 2012 study done by the Ryerson University Sleep and Depression Lab discovered that 46 percent of the people surveyed who reported insomnia also were afraid of the dark.[3]

I am amazed to see what secular scientists hypothesize as possible causes for fear of the dark. In his article "Why Are We Afraid of the Dark?" Mansal Denton identified three possible unrelated reasons. The first possible cause, according to Denton, could be a subconscious throwback to our early history as human beings, when we were vulnerable at night to predatory animals. A second link comes from his agreement with Freud's belief that fear of darkness is related to separation anxiety from our mother. Somehow the pain of separation at night became a fear of the night when we experienced loneliness. Finally, this nighttime fear is possibly related to the belief some people have that they are more likely to experience crime at night. This is a fear based on ignorance of the fact that an equal number of crimes are committed during the day as during the night.[4]

Although these are thought-provoking ideas, I believe ignorance and deception are far more powerful reasons for anxiety at night than wanting my mommy or being afraid a wild tiger is going to attack me as I sleep. The perpetrator of the deception is none other than Satan—the father of lies. He is also called the devil, which means "slanderer or deceiver." He knows Scripture and uses it to bring doubt and confusion by twisting it. Eve was confronted by the serpent's tempting question, "Did God really say . . . ?" (Genesis 3:1 NLT). His purpose is always to slander God and portray himself as equal to or more powerful than God.

I did not realize until I began doing research for this book that he had duped me, too. The discovery of this trick came as I researched several phrases that I knew were in the Bible; I just could not remember where. When my online concordance did not give me the reference for "prince of darkness," I took my search to Google. No success. There was no reference to

Satan as "prince of darkness." And other than the New Living Translation, neither is there a reference to the "kingdom of darkness," which I was positive was in Colossians 1:13, where Paul wrote about our being translated into the Kingdom of God's dear Son. Although I am not a Greek scholar, I believe the translators of the New Living Translation, whether influenced by the myth of the "prince of darkness" or simply trying to make a literary comparison between God's Kingdom of light and the enemy's area of influence, did not accurately convey the meaning of that verse. Satan does not have a kingdom; he simply has power to influence the minds of people through lies, drawing them away from God's Kingdom of light into *spiritual* darkness, not a *literal* place over which Satan exerts authority.

I found articles written about the "kingdom of darkness," but no Bible reference in the articles for that phrase. What I did find was a pop culture use of those terms, which began with a sermon by a priest, Bernard of Clairvaux, in the twelfth century. John Milton used this phrase again in his seventeenth-century poem "Paradise Lost."[5] In the nineteenth century, Bram Stoker wrote the horror novel *Dracula*, which was followed by the twentieth-century horror film *Dracula: Prince of Darkness*. Later, Alice Cooper released an album called *Prince of Darkness*, and Ozzy Osbourne cut a set of CDs called by the same name.[6]

It is easy to see how a misquote of Scripture, brought to life by pop culture, would lead to the belief that Satan is the prince of darkness. If Satan were the prince of darkness and the ruler of the kingdom of darkness, the logical conclusion would be that the night/darkness is his territory and the light/daytime is God's domain. Who would not be nervous—even panicked—to go to sleep at night as a trespasser in the enemy's kingdom? I doubt many soldiers fighting behind enemy lines experience sweet, undisturbed sleep at night, and neither do we if we believe we are sleeping in enemy territory.

The Truth about Darkness

The truth about the darkness is revealed in Genesis 1:1–5. It was from darkness that God began the work of creation. The writer describes this event in verses 1–2: "In the beginning God created the heavens and the earth. The earth was without form, and void; and darkness was on the face of the deep. And the Spirit of God was hovering over the face of the waters." Picture this scene, although it is difficult to picture because it was dark! But God was there, in the darkness. Imagine you are alone in the middle of a pitch-black desert—no stars, no moon and no streetlights, just blackness. Suddenly you hear a voice saying, "Light, be!" You did not know anyone was there because you could not see Him, but He was there all the time, in the dark. And even more astounding, He could control the darkness because He controlled the light. Whoever owns the light also owns the darkness.

God showed His ownership of both the light and the darkness because He not only divided one from the other, but then He named the light *day* and the darkness He called *night*. Whoever names a thing has authority over it. Night was never an oppositional force against light. There was not a cosmic battle between God's light and the darkness. Together the light and the darkness, that 24-hour period, composed the first day. According to Genesis 1:5, "the evening and the morning were the first day." Instead of nighttime being a time of anxiety to endure till dawn, it was the beginning of the day. It was the time of preparation for the daylight hours through rest and interaction with God during sleep. In God's mind, there never was, nor ever has been, any doubt about who owns the darkness. Isaiah reported God's emphatic statement to the people: "I form the light and create darkness" (Isaiah 45:7).

Throughout the Scriptures there is confirmation of the truth that God owns, as well as dwells in, the darkness. When God summoned Moses to meet with Him on Mount Sinai, Scripture describes the scene of the meeting: "Moses drew near the thick darkness where God was" (Exodus 20:21). God demonstrated His ownership of darkness when He gave Moses power to release the ninth plague of three days of thick darkness over the land of Egypt as an encouragement to Pharaoh to set God's people free. This was not ordinary darkness caused by an eclipse. The dark was so thick people felt it and could not even see one another, but that was only in Egypt. The Israelites continued to enjoy life as usual in Goshen, where they lived (see Exodus 10:22–23). David confirmed God's presence in the darkness in Psalm 97:2, when he described the scene around God as "clouds and darkness." His son Solomon quoted God's declaration that He "would dwell in the thick darkness" (1 Kings 8:12 KJV).

History-Making in the Darkness

Other than creation, the most historic event in the darkness occurred two thousand years ago, in a stable in the remote town of Bethlehem (see Matthew 2:1). God loves to hide things, even in the dark, so that His children have the joy of discovery, a never-ending eternal treasure hunt laid out by the Father Himself. This was His most precious treasure, birthed at night. The birth coaches were the animals mooing and bleating near the manger as Mary delivered the King, the long-awaited Savior of the world. This will always be the most famous birth of all time.

God uses the most insignificant people and places for significant impact. This event tops that list of insignificant places. Who in the world but God would choose darkness as the stage to reveal the Light of the world? To Him who is the Light, there is no darkness, so it does not matter. He used the darkness from which to orchestrate such a pageant of glory, bringing together the angel choir and the stars as headliners for the show. He had left clues through the centuries for treasure seekers, even for those who were not followers of God. The Magi knew the star that night was not like the other stars. They had no access to the Hubble Space Telescope to help identify what they were looking at. Names did not matter. The magnetic pull from that star carried them through the countryside, to light their way to the birthplace of this holy night's main attraction—King Jesus.

Given the overwhelming evidence of God's creation of and activity in the darkness, it would appear people are mistaken if they believe Satan owns it, because it is not possible for both God and the devil to own and control the darkness. Perhaps you have been confused, just as I was, about the darkness. As we have seen, some of the confusion about its ownership stemmed from one phrase used by a priest in the twelfth century, "prince of darkness." This phrase was perpetuated through the ages, with help from the media through books, movies and video games. Even some Christians today are purveyors of these falsehoods because of a lack of teaching or careless study. The enemy loves to see the power of lies rob us of our sleep.

Literal and Figurative Darkness

There are several different words in Hebrew and Greek meaning dark or darkness, either literally or figuratively, depending on the context. The readers of the Bible who knew Hebrew or Greek understood the words *dark* or *darkness* could mean actual physical darkness, or they could mean spiritual darkness. Unfortunately, the English translation of these words does not make a distinction between darkness of the night and darkness caused by spiritual blindness.

For example, one Hebrew word for darkness, *choshek*, used in Genesis 1:5 to refer to the literal darkness that God called *night*, is the same word used in Isaiah 9:2, where the writer refers to the concept that "the people who walked in darkness have seen a great light." This verse means the people were living in spiritual darkness, not literal darkness, but it is translated simply as "darkness," not "spiritual darkness." Because of sin, they were cut off from God, the source of spiritual light. Paul describes this condition as a darkened heart, the result of not glorifying or giving thanks to God (see Romans 1:21). The end result of this figurative darkness is spiritual death.

Each of these words in the original language may have a figurative rather than a literal meaning. Without careful examination of these Scriptures—and if a person's bias is to believe that Satan is the prince of a kingdom of darkness—it is easy to add fuel to the fear of darkness.

The result of a darkened heart is intellectual darkness (see Romans 2:19), which results in "works of darkness" (Ephesians 5:11). Such works refer not to evil done in the literal darkness, but to activities influenced by the lies of Satan and the selfish desires of the soul separated from God. Following such a path makes individuals figuratively children of darkness—people who from generation to generation choose to disobey God, becoming spiritually blind.

If you are physically blind, your world is dark. But spiritual darkness is a state of heart and mind, not a geographical location. The punishment for those who don't repent (change their way of thinking) is life in an eternal state of spiritual darkness, and therefore separation from God, who is the Light. Wherever God sends them to geographically on Judgment Day, wherever they spend eternity, whether it is called Hades, the lake of fire, or outer darkness, it all belongs to God. It was created by Him and is under *His* dominion—all of it! This is the important point for winning the battle for the night—understanding that God created, dwells in and has authority over *all* the darkness. He is allowing the darkness of the present world, caused by the evil deeds of people living in spiritual blindness, to continue until the Day of Judgment, to give each person time to repent.

Because the influence of the lies about darkness has been so pervasive, some of the truths about it have been passed over or even ignored. After our examination of some of these Scripture references, we now know the truth that God dwells in the darkness. It is a mystery that the One who is Light lives in darkness, but the Scripture also describes Him as being invisible. If you dwelt in darkness you would probably be invisible, but not if you were also light. That thought could keep you awake at night, trying to figure it out.

God's Secret Place

Rather than go round and round in a mystery, I would like to focus on truths about God in the darkness that are easy to comprehend. Psalm 27:5 is a favorite. David had a lot of experience with trouble, but he was strengthened by his confidence that God would hide him in His pavilion, in the secret place of His Tabernacle. As children, my friend Arnie and I imagined ourselves in the midst of a hostile world, in need of a hideout, a secret place. When the imaginary bad guys were after us, we hopped on our two-wheel bikes and raced down the alley, across the street, through a break in the bushes, to a narrow path down a steep hill. No one knew that the rock in the middle of the path marked the entrance to our fortress. We were sworn to secrecy; our lives depended on it.

The difference between our secret place and the one David knew about is that according to Psalm 18:11, God chose to make darkness His secret place. Our hideout was in broad daylight. For safety, I think darkness would probably be a better location, particularly if God was there. Isaiah also received revelation about God hiding His treasures in the darkness (see Isaiah 45:3).

If you want to hide something, it makes sense that you would put it somewhere out of sight. Darkness would be a good choice. David enjoyed not only safety in God's pavilion in the dark, but also God's gift to him of the treasures of darkness and the hidden riches of His secret place—darkness.

Is it any wonder that Satan has been on a major deception campaign to rob us not only of the sleep our body needs, but also of the treasures God wants to give us at night as we sleep? Solomon knew that even if his body was asleep, his heart was awake to receive instruction, wisdom, or the dreams, revelation or songs in the night that Job spoke about (see Job 35:10). It is time to take back the night.

Safe in the Dark

At a conference, I taught these truths about God owning and dwelling in the darkness. The attendees stood at the end of the session and declared these truths out loud. (These declarations are in the appendix, so we will look at them in more detail later.) The next day, a lady excitedly reported to me her experience on the previous night, after she had heard the message on God and the darkness. Sheepishly, she told me she had slept with a light on her entire life because of her fear of the dark. The night she came home from the conference, however, she told her husband she wanted to turn off the light.

After eleven years of marriage sleeping with the light on, her husband knew something significant had happened to his wife. They went to bed, this time in the dark. The lady told me she woke up once in the night and felt some anxiety, but then she remembered the truth she had learned and boldly declared at the conference: "God, You own the night! You dwell in the darkness!" She sat up in bed, repeated that declaration, rolled over and fell back to sleep.

Prayer

God, thank You for the truth that You, as Creator of the darkness, have authority over it and dwell in it. When I go to sleep at night, I am not in enemy territory, but am resting in Your secret place. There is no need to be afraid in the dark, because You are there as the King, ruling over both the day and the night, and I am safe.

The Enemy's Tactics

8

He disarmed the spiritual rulers
and authorities. He shamed them publicly
by his victory over them on the cross.

Colossians 2:15 NLT

It is not enough to know God's plan and promises for the night and the benefits they impart to us, and to observe His nighttime activity in biblical history. We must be aware of the enemy's tactics to rob us physically, mentally and spiritually of God's provision for us during sleep. The goal of the CIA, FBI, MI5 and every military and intelligence officer is to discover the tactics of the enemy. Knowledge is the key to victory.

According to the Bible, the demons not only know the Scriptures, but also believe them and tremble (see James 2:19). Although God does not reveal His timing, He has not hidden His plans and promises from Satan, who knows the historic events that took place while Adam, Abraham, Jacob, David, Solomon and Joseph slept. Satan is troubled by the power generated by the Father's love directed to the human soul during sleep. He knows love wins every time.

Satan's goal is to rob God's children of the gift of peaceful sleep, blocking the nighttime transfer of treasure, provision, promise and strategies through dreams, downloads and songs of love. He has developed numerous methods of accomplishing this. He is a master thief. It is time to expose his three major tactics.

Everywhere, we see evidence of the enemy's tactics. Many people are being robbed every night and don't even know it. They may have security systems or a shotgun under the bed. Neither is a deterrent to this thief who comes in the night. Without recognizing the robber's MO, it is difficult to be protected from him. We have already examined the statistics about rampant insomnia and its effects.[1] Satan has turned God's peaceful dwelling place of darkness into enemy territory—a place of anxiety, fear and terror for many people. Their only peace often comes through prescription drugs, illegal drugs, alcohol or other mind-numbing activities.[2] There is no condemnation intended in that statement. It is the enemy who is our focus in this chapter. To stop him, we must find out how he operates.

Tactic #1—Lies

Jesus identified Satan as the father of lies (see John 8:44). The source of his power and influence stems from deception. The danger of deception is its deceptiveness. Sounds obvious, I know. Just because it is does not mean we are not affected by the reality of it. We saw in the last chapter the power of the lies about darkness, which robs people of peaceful sleep at night. Those lies would not have such power if they were not coupled with deception about Satan's power. I talk with many believers whose lives reflect the influence of the enemy's lies about his power and authority. In such cases, although a person may recite Scriptures about being more than a conqueror, his or her daily experience does not demonstrate those declarations.

The disarming of Satan

From Genesis through Revelation, one message comes through loud and clear—Satan is not equal to God. The Bible is the testament of God's love and power in redeeming His children from punishment for sin. He did it through the sacrifice of Jesus on the cross as payment for the sins of the whole world, thus stripping Satan of the legal right he had to make accusations against us. Jesus was sent on a mission to earth to "destroy the works of the devil" (1 John 3:8). With a final declaration of "It is finished!" from the cross, He told His Father He had completed His assignment (John 19:30). Included in that statement is the fulfillment of the words He had spoken to His disciples just prior to His crucifixion—"now the ruler of this world will be cast out" (John 12:31).

Paul carries on this testimony of Jesus' victory through His death, burial and resurrection with these words: "Having disarmed principalities and powers, He made a public spectacle of them, triumphing over them in it" (Colossians 2:15). This sounds to me as though someone suffered a complete rout, and it was not God!

You may be thinking perhaps the devil was resurrected along with Jesus, because he seems alive and well on the earth. That is what Satan wants us to believe. Jesus told His disciples He had all power and all authority. If He has it all, that makes it impossible for Satan to have any. And yet it seems as if he does. How does he get his arms of power back if Jesus *disarmed* him? Simple: Every time we believe his lies, we rearm him. His power came through accusation and deception. Jesus took care of the accusations by offering Himself as payment to God for our debt of sin, but we have to continue to combat the power of the enemy's lies with truth.

Think of the large blow-up Santa in your neighbor's yard at Christmas. It is the one in the middle of all the other displays, taller than the roof, lit up by ten thousand lights bouncing to "Jingle Bells" piped through car radios. The giant Santa rules the display at night. In the morning, there is no sign of Santa. Oops, there he is—a rubberized puddle in the middle of the yard. What happened? Someone pulled the plug on his power to tower in the yard. Jesus pulled the plug on Satan on the cross. We blow him back up and empower him to dominate the yard when we believe his lies.

The truth about our wrestling match

One example of distorted thinking about Satan is the verse "We do not wrestle against flesh and blood, but against principalities, against powers, against the rulers of the darkness of this age, against spiritual hosts of wickedness in the heavenly places" (Ephesians 6:12). From that one verse the devil has persuaded people to become professional demon wrestlers, getting pummeled and bloodied in the ring, doing all they can to help Jesus win the cosmic battle between light and darkness. They forget that *Jesus already won.*

I believe Paul did not need to write *disarmed* principalities and powers in Ephesians 6:12, because the early Church understood the full ramifications of the death, burial and resurrection of Jesus Christ. Paul had already told the Ephesians that they were seated in heavenly places, far above all principality and power and might and dominion (see Ephesians 2:6). These are the same principalities and powers he described in Colossians 2:15, where he stated that Jesus "disarmed principalities and powers" and "made a public spectacle of them, triumphing over them in it [the cross]."

The wrestling match, as envisioned by Paul, involved a disarmed opponent who is under, beneath, below us. Anyone who has ever watched a wrestling match knows the person on top, above his opponent, has the advantage. An opponent underneath, particularly one whose body has no arms, is the loser before the match even begins. In the physical, we would never see this kind of match because wrestling with an opponent who has no arms is ludicrous. But in the spiritual, the enemy tricks us into a fight by lying to us about his ability to fight. He knows he has been disarmed, but he keeps taunting us, trying to get us to engage. When we take the bait, we rearm him. Don't take the bait!

Our protective armor

If Satan is powerless and the battle is not the hand-to-hand combat we have envisioned, you may wonder why we need the armor Paul described later, in Ephesians 6. The only weapons the devil has left to use against us are his words, all of which are lies. First Peter 5:8–9 describes the enemy as a roaring lion that we are to resist through standing firm in the faith. The lion's roars are his words. The weapon we use against the roaring lies of the enemy is the truth of the Word of God.

A close look at the pieces of the armor in Ephesians 6 reveals that their purpose is to protect us from and equip us for a battle against lies about God, the devil and ourselves. Our job is to stand, shielded against intimidation, temptation and accusation by the armor of God that consists of faith, hope, peace and the righteousness of Christ.

The battlefield is our mind, and the war is waged between the fiery darts (lies) of the enemy and the sword of the Spirit (truth of the Word of God). If the truth of the Bible sets us free, the lies of the enemy have the power to bind us up. In the next chapter we will learn how to wield the weapon of truth.

Tactic #2—Fear

Lies often produce fear, which then empowers the lies. Fear is a form of faith—faith in a lie rather than in the truth. Faith is powerful, even if misplaced. Fear, an empowered lie, is one of the primary tactics of the enemy's nighttime thievery.

Let's take a look at what fear looks like today. The word *fear* is still used in church vernacular and in society. I have observed in myself and in other people that we seem to use the word *anxiety* when we want to make it sound as if we are facing a "normal" fear, or a fear with less intensity. We also use this term when people have a debilitating condition that they believe is an unchangeable part of their life. It seems that we use *anxiety*, then, to describe everything from a minor feeling of fear to a disorder that requires medication.

How prevalent is fear? Anxiety and anxiety-related disorders are common, at least in American society. According to the National Institutes of Health, roughly 18 percent of adults in the country I live in suffer from some type of anxiety disorder such as traumatic stress, generalized anxiety (marked by excessive worrying), panic and phobias.[3] Other studies cite that roughly 57 million Americans have a diagnosed anxiety disorder,[4] and 37 percent of those are receiving some sort of treatment for the anxiety.[5] Among children and adolescents, estimates of those who suffer anxiety are between 15 and 20 percent of the U.S. population.[6]

A substantial portion of the population here in the United States is dealing with some form of anxiety that hinders quality of life. In some instances, individuals are completely debilitated by their fear. Remember, these statistics only account for those who might have some type of anxiety-related diagnosis. These numbers don't take into account the people who battle fear without seeking help.

The effects of fear on the body

Because we are body, soul and spirit, when fear increases, there is a literal effect on the body. In one publication from Harvard Medical School, "Anxiety and Physical Illness," the authors note that anxiety is often the underlying source for many other physical conditions and addictions.[7] Some of these conditions might include migraines, irritable bowel syndrome and disorders where pain is experienced but a physical source cannot be identified.

This same report cites emerging evidence of the relationship between digestive issues, chronic respiratory conditions and the development of heart and coronary disease.

The effects of fear on the brain

Moreover, those suffering with fear and anxiety are often experiencing other types of symptoms. The most recent manual for psychological diagnoses noted the close relationship between major depression and a generalized anxiety disorder.[8] That is, anxiety often is not experienced alone; rather, it is experienced alongside depression. Anxiety and depression are often found with insomnia, although it is not clear if one condition is causing the other.[9] The bottom line is that fear weighs us down and causes us to lose sleep, which is the goal of the enemy—to rob us of God's gift of rest.

The effects of fear can be seen when it comes to our experience of major traumas. When certain traumas such as rape occur, nearly everyone will experience traumatic stress symptoms (apart from a miracle).[10] These life-threatening, fearful and traumatic events have the potential to reshape our brains. Research is clear about what happens to a person's brain in response to a significant traumatic event. The person exposed to this type of trauma may experience unwanted and intrusive thoughts, may feel guilt, shame and anger, and may have nightmares and physical symptoms related to the event(s).[11] But just as physical problems stemming from lack of sleep can be healed, emotional problems arising from traumatic events can also be healed. Remember, God is the God of hope, and nothing is impossible with Him (see Romans 15:13; Mark 10:27).

Fear and nighttime traumas

Under cover of darkness, which many still erroneously believe to be the devil's kingdom, scary events occur, sinful acts perpetrated by human beings. U.S. Department of Justice statistics note that the majority of rapes occur between the hours of 6 p.m. and midnight, and another 24 percent occur between midnight and 6 a.m., particularly in the lives of children. Studies reveal that 67 percent of sexual assaults occur between 6 p.m. and 6 a.m.[12] This includes assaults on adults as well as children.

After such traumas these individuals never see night as a safe time, apart from God's intervention. According to one study cited in the *Journal of Pediatric Psychology*, "Sexual abuse compromises sleep safety because it often occurs at night in a place where the child must continue to sleep after being abused and/or during periods of ongoing abuse."[13] These experiences can open a door to fear, which the enemy then uses night after night. I want to assure you that no matter what trauma you have endured at night, God can restore peaceful sleep to you, beginning tonight.

Fear and the media's fuel for nightmares

Another place we see fear gain entrance into our life is through movies and video games. We have movies of demons and monsters chasing an unsuspecting college student into a dark abandoned house. Then there are our societal tales of the boogeyman under the bed or the monster in the closet. Children are told fairy tales about wolves pretending to be grandmas—stories that would horrify any sensitive adult. The list goes on of haunted houses and scary rides where some people actually pay money for the possibility of being frightened into soiling their undergarments. In fact, the combined gross receipts of the top 20 horror films released in 2013 and 2014 were over $2.5 billion worldwide.[14] That is a lot of cash spent, all for an accelerated heart rate and sweaty palms!

The enemy continues his torment of fear with nightmares. The word *nightmare* means "night demon." The dreams we have that feel as if they came from the pit of hell actually did. Because we often think of nightmares as something primarily children experience, as adults we may be ashamed to admit that we have nightmares. Yet studies show that nightmares are not reserved for children alone. The same article I already quoted from the *Journal of Pediatric Psychology* also reported this:

> Research on adult sexual assault has shown that upward of 77% of survivors report insomnia, nightmares, sleep-disordered breathing, and/or sleep-related movement disorders and that suffering from sleep problems likely persists for many years after the initial trauma.[15]

The torment someone experiences from the enemy at night may be a result of the person's victimization. The devil does not care. He is relentless. Other fears may harass us through our own choices. The horror movie we paid to see, the gory novel we read or the violent video game we play may all be vehicles he uses. We are not wired for nerve-racking fear. There is a difference between the weapon of fear the devil uses against us and the holy fear of the Lord inspired by an encounter with an omnipotent God. We will not experience the fulfillment of Jesus' prayer for heaven on earth if Satan is allowed to torment us through fear. God has given us a weapon that is more powerful than fear. In the next chapter, we will see how powerful it is against Satan.

Tactic #3—Fantasy

Lies and fears are not the enemy's only tactics. His goal is to capture the screening room of our brain by substituting fantasies for dreams. There is only one screen, and it was designed as the place where God would show us heavenly visions. We are to "see" the screen with spiritual eyes. One online article about visual stimulation reported that 60 percent of our entire brain is used for seeing.[16] Modern marketing capitalizes on this fact. Hollywood producers are masters of visual stimuli. Unfortunately, many of their movie scenes are tools the enemy uses to capture the screen of our brain through violence and promiscuity. Poet and author Allen Ginsberg stated, "Whoever controls the media—the images—controls the culture."[17]

Pornography—a dream robber

Even more troubling are the statistics on pornography. Here are just a few pornography statistics from 2012, and the numbers have no doubt increased since that time. These are taken from an article entitled "Internet Pornography by the Numbers":

- 40 million Americans regularly visit porn sites.
- 2.5 billion emails sent or received every day contain porn.[18]

Eric Dye, in his 2012 *ChurchMag* article, lists further tragic statistics about the growing pornography curse:

- 90 percent of children ages 8–16 have viewed pornography.
- $10 billion to $14 billion is spent on porn annually—the amount the government spends on foreign aid.[19]

I do not present these statistics as condemnation or to increase shame. I am including these statistics for the sole purpose of exposing the enemy's tactics. The goal is to enable believers to take back their night and enjoy God's presence with them as they sleep.

Scientific studies have shown the deleterious effects of pornography on the brain. A 2012 article in *Live Science* entitled "Porn May Shut Down Part of Your Brain" states that "new research finds that looking at erotic movies can actually quiet the part of the brain that processes visual stimuli."[20] This statement confirms the premise that the enemy's tactic is to hinder God's dream downloads to the screen of our brain by tempting us to fill the screen with pornographic images. This choice may result in shutting down our capacity to receive the visual stimuli of the dreams.

Pornography is the fuel the brain uses to fantasize. The word *fantasy* comes from the Middle English word *fantasie*, meaning "imaginative faculty, mental image."[21] The Greek origin of the word is *phantasia*, defined as an idea, notion and image. The capacity to have imaginative mental images is God-given. It is the material we choose as data to put on the mental imaging screen that creates the problem.

Deliverance from fantasy

Not all fantasy has sexual content. I heard the testimony of a woman who used fantasy as a form of comfort. Her nighttime fantasies had no sexual innuendos. If she had had a challenging day, did not feel affirmed or had failed in some task, comfort came as she entered into a fantasy world at night where she was the superhero, the champion, with crowds cheering. Yet she was frustrated at her lack of God dreams.

Everyone around this woman had testimonies of life-changing night visions. She believed that as a strong Christian, she should be having the same nighttime experiences. Once again, hunger and curiosity were the keys to revelation and freedom. She asked God the "why" question: *Why don't I dream at night?*

God told her, *You don't dream because you fantasize.*

No one had ever preached to her about fantasy, and there did not seem to be any Scriptures about not fantasizing. Yet God was implying that the activity was a substitute for His dreams. She was willing to stop immediately if it meant her dream life would begin.

This woman was surprised when the revelation of the truth did not provide the immediate results she was hoping for. She discovered that there was a battle for the movie theater in her mind. The enemy did not want to give up occupancy of that screening room. Each night, she said *no* to fantasy and invited the Holy Spirit to occupy the projection room. Her dreams did not begin right away; it took some time, but she now has God-inspired dreams on a regular basis. She also knows God's impartation to her while she sleeps is not always through a dream. It may also come in the form of downloads to her spirit, which she will not "see," but will understand and experience at a later time, as needed.

We Are Not Defenseless

God has not left us defenseless against the enemy's tactics of lies, fear and fantasy. If we have suffered wounds from the devil's activity, whether as a result of someone else's behavior or through our own unwise choices, God can heal every physical, mental or emotional trauma we have experienced.

Unfortunately, we live in a society that has embraced a victim mentality. A victim mindset is one of helplessness, which produces hopelessness. Satan loves this! It is based on a lie that empowers him to continue to torment us with additional lies and fears.

The Gospel, the Good News, is a victorious message of hope that brings redemption and restoration. No situation is impossible with God. In the next chapter, we will learn the power of our weapons against the adversary.

Prayer

Father, thank You that no matter what I have suffered at the hands of the enemy through the sins of others, or even through my own decision to believe his lies, yield to fear or open a door to him through fantasy, You make all things new. I am not a victim. Rather, according to Your Word I can be forgiven, healed and set free. I am more than a conqueror!

Weapons to Win the Battle

For the weapons of our warfare are . . . mighty in God.

2 Corinthians 10:4

Congratulations for making it this far through the book! We have seen the ravages of the enemy's war at night as he uses his weapons of lies, fear and fantasy to attempt to rob us of God's presence and provision as we sleep. This chapter is where we learn to use our three weapons to win the battle. (Note: Reader participation is required! For real change to occur, something more than reading a book must happen.)

Because I grew up in a Christian home, read lots of books at an early age and went to church and conferences, I thought I was experiencing the reality of life with God. Then I began to learn the difference between knowing about God the Father and actually having a heart connection and communication with Him on a daily basis. Rather than just knowing Bible verses about prayer, in order for prayer to work in my life I had to pray.

That seems obvious, but with the rise of secular humanism—a religion of the mind—the temptation is to live our beliefs through our intellect rather than through fellowship with the Holy Spirit. It is the Word of God, together with the Spirit of God, that makes the Word more than an intellectual exercise. Jesus demonstrated this principle. People were astonished because His words stopped storms, sent demons running, healed the sick, multiplied food and even raised the dead. Because we have become conditioned to words without power, we have less expectation that there will be any change at all when we pray or make a declaration of truth. It is time to live beyond the borders of our intellect through partnership with the Holy Spirit.

The Weapon of Truth

In our arsenal of weapons to win the battle for the night, truth is the first weapon that deactivates every lie of Satan. I know that sounds simplistic. If we analyze the Gospel message and compare it to other religions or philosophies, it is the simplest of them all. Jesus boiled down His message to this statement: "I am the way, the truth, and the life" (John 14:6). Truth is the key to life; a full life lived in freedom, wholeness and physical health. Jesus Christ is the way to that truth. He was the embodiment of everything that God is, and all God's promises were packed into His life and demonstrated on earth. Everything He said and did was to reverse the insinuation of God's flawed character that the serpent floated to Eve in the Garden (see Genesis 3:1).

Eve and Adam had an idyllic life with each other and with God in a paradise created just for them and their offspring for eternity. It was perfect in every detail, prepared by their loving Creator Father. The serpent had only one weapon to destroy this enviable environment—a lie. He did not come out and say, "God has lied to you." That would have been too direct, and Eve would have shot it down with the truth. Instead, he opened the door to a lie through doubt. His question to her was, "Did God really say . . . ?" (Genesis 3:1 NLT).

Eve made the mistake of choosing doubt rather than rebutting the lie with truth. If she had answered the serpent with what God said rather than allowing room for doubt, the painful story of the end of their life in paradise would not have occurred. Truth would have silenced the lie the serpent was trying to plant in her heart about God's lack of love and faithfulness.

The battle for truth began that day and continues to this day. The Old Testament prophet Isaiah said, "Truth is fallen in the street" (Isaiah 59:14). Pontius Pilate, when he was interrogating Jesus, asked, "What is truth?" (John 18:38). In Psalm 119:160 (KJV), David said, "Thy word is truth." Paul said that God "upholds all things by the word of His power" (Hebrews 1:3 NASB). Putting those last two Scriptures together means that the world, which was formed by the word of God, was formed by truth. Satan's intent has been to destroy God's Kingdom through lies. It was and is a battle of truth over lies.

Jesus and the Weapon of Truth

Jesus demonstrated the power of the weapon of truth against the devil during His forty-day fast in the desert. He was sent not only to destroy the works of the devil, but also to reveal the Father (see John 14:9) and to model how we are to live as sons and daughters of God, empowered by the Holy Spirit (see Romans 8:29; 1 John 4:17). Although He was the Son of God and could have asked His Father to send an army of angels to help Him in the desert, just as He could have done from the cross (see Matthew 26:53), He chose to use a weapon just as powerful in defeating the enemy as an army of angels—the truth of the Word of God. Each of the three times the devil attacked Him with a temptation based on a lie, Jesus countered the assault with the words "It is written," followed by a Scripture verse (see Matthew 4:3–11). After the enemy's third attempt to lure Jesus into sin, Matthew reports "the devil left Him" (verse 11). Truth is a powerful weapon!

It is not enough to have the weapon; we need to learn how to use it. Men and women in the armed services are issued weapons to protect themselves and win the battle against the enemy. Their instructors know the lives of the soldiers depend on more than wearing revolvers in holsters strapped to their legs. They must be trained to use the gun and practice what they are taught. They spend hours every day at the practice range, learning to hit the target. We have been issued our weapon, too: "the sword of the Spirit, which is the word of God" (Ephesians 6:17). It is time to learn to use it.

Just as soldiers use a laser to locate the target, the Holy Spirit will show us our target, which is each falsehood that the enemy has hurled at us. Once a deception has been identified, the first step in eradicating it is to renounce it out loud. Remember, this is a battle of words—ours against the roars of the enemy. If we have allowed his lie to become part of a mindset in our thinking, we need to renew our mind. Repudiating the lie out loud, and replacing it with a verbal declaration of the truth, triggers our mind's renewal and transformation process that Paul described in 2 Corinthians 10:5 and Romans 12:2. God demonstrated the power of words with His first declaration: "Light, be!" (see Genesis 1:3; Hebrews 11:3). Solomon confirmed the power of words when he wrote, "Death and life are in the power of the tongue" (Proverbs 18:21).

Weapons Training

Now is the time for you to practice using this weapon of truth against some of the lies the enemy has told about the darkness and night. Take a few minutes to do the following exercise, using the truths shown in the chart to counter the lies listed next to them.

For the first one, start by saying out loud, "I repent for believing the lie that Satan owns the darkness," and then say, "I renounce the lie that Satan owns the darkness."

Replace the lie by repeating the truth next to it: "God created the darkness and therefore owns it."

Go through each of the lies and truths in the list, speaking a renunciation of each lie and a declaration of each truth.

LIE	TRUTH
Satan owns the darkness.	God created the darkness and therefore owns it.
I am not safe in the darkness because it belongs to Satan.	I am safe in the darkness because it belongs to God.
I need to be on guard at night because bad things happen in the dark.	God is with me at night, so I can sleep. His angels watch over me.
I never sleep peacefully at night and never will. It is hopeless.	God gives me, His beloved, peaceful sleep.
Fear overpowers me at night.	God, who is perfect love, overpowers and casts out fear.

There may be other lies you have believed about the night. Take a few minutes and ask God to show you those lies, along with the truths that disempower them. Once the lies are identified, repent of and renounce them, and then confess the truths God shows you. The list of declarations in the appendix may be helpful to turn to for more statements of truth. One key to winning the battle for the night is to cultivate an awareness of the enemy-whispered lies in your ear and silence him immediately with the truth.

Dealing with Doubt and Condemnation

Using the weapon of truth successfully is not just a matter of the mouth uttering words. There is a connection between the heart and those words. Until I learned this, I struggled with the idea of making declarations of truth. I knew the Bible was full of instructions about using our voice, lips and mouth to declare, preach, sing and shout the truth of God. The problem for me was feeling hypocritical. I might have said the right things, but sometimes I felt something different on the inside that bordered on doubt. My mouth was saying one thing, but inside I was hearing things like these:

This will never work.

I doubt this is really true.

I am not worthy of this happening to me.

I did not realize it was necessary for my heart to be in agreement with my mouth in order to feel confident about the outcome.

The New Testament writer of 1 John 3:21–22 diagnosed my problem when he wrote, "If our heart does not condemn us, we have confidence toward God. And whatever we ask we receive from Him." The reason I had little or no confidence in the words I was speaking was that I had condemnation in my heart. The condemnation was the source of my doubt; its presence was draining my confidence little by little.

The meaning of the Bible word *condemn* is "to find fault with, blame," or "to accuse."[1] This fault-finding may be toward others, but most likely is toward myself. Wherever I am holding on to guilt, I am partnering with condemnation. It is guilty people who are subject to a judge's verdict of punishment. Being sentenced to prison is another way of saying being condemned because of breaking the law, which requires punishment.

The antidote to condemnation is forgiveness. The Good News of the Gospel is that Jesus, through His sacrificial death on the cross, took on Himself the punishment of death for all the sins of the human race from the beginning of time. That is the reason Paul wrote, "There is therefore now no condemnation to those who are in Christ Jesus" (Romans 8:1). The power of forgiveness through Jesus Christ is the only power that releases us from the punishment that we are due. Satan is empowered to torment us with accusatory lies if we do not accept the truth of our acquittal, but hold on to our rap sheet.

The Weapon of Forgiveness

The foundation of the Christian life is built on forgiveness and sustained by the daily practice of it toward others and toward myself. Jesus confirmed this truth in the prayer He taught His disciples (see Matthew 6:9–13). The emphasis in the prayer is on the daily experience of receiving bread from the Father, as well as forgiving others and receiving forgiveness. The disciples wanted to get further explanation about how many times they needed to forgive someone. Their thought was that 7 times would be plenty, but Jesus rocked their thinking by multiplying that by 70. Yikes! Was that 490 times in a day, a week, a year, maybe a lifetime? If we think about that number in light of our own self-accusations, however, it does not seem so outrageous.

Although forgiveness is the cornerstone of the Christian life, I meet a shocking number of Christians harboring unforgiveness. For some, their bitterness is the result of horrific abuse, while others allow guilt to feed unforgiveness toward themselves. The trickiest form of resentment to deal with is the kind against God Himself. If God is perfect, how can I forgive Him? (We will talk more about that shortly.)

Jesus made it clear that forgiveness is required. The commandment is not for God's sake, but for ours. Matthew 18 paints a vivid picture of the painful results of unforgiveness. Because of unwillingness to forgive a small debt in spite of having been forgiven a huge one, the man in the story is put in prison and turned over to the tormentors. The word *tormentors* is used only once in the entire New Testament. That fact attracts my attention. According to the *Blue Letter Bible* lexicon online, the Greek word for *tormentors* is *basanistes*. It is defined as "one who elicits the truth by the use of the rack," and also "an inquisitor, torturer also used of a jailer doubtless because the business of torturing was also assigned to him."[2]

This description of the tormentor makes me shudder inside. The thought of torture on a rack is frightening. Even more alarming than the mechanics of the experience is the awareness of the unfeeling evilness of the person performing the torture. Paul told the Ephesians in chapter 4, verse 26 not to let the sun go down on their anger. The New Living Translation gives a clear reason for dealing with anger before darkness falls in verse 27: "for anger gives a foothold to the devil." Unresolved anger at night turns on a bright spotlight, with a loud megaphone that blares into the air, *Calling all demons!*

To me, the choice between forgiving or holding on to anger is a no-brainer. Regardless of the offense, disappointment, betrayal, abuse, I would let it go rather than invite heartless, torture-loving demons to share my bed because I chose not to forgive before going to sleep.

Grace to Forgive

For some, the act of forgiveness seems impossible because of the horrific nature of the offense against them. It is not always easy, partly because sometimes our idea of what forgiveness involves is not true. Here are some things forgiveness is not:

- It is not saying the other person was right, and I was wrong.
- It is not giving the person permission to do it again.
- It is not living without any boundaries with the person.
- It is not saying the offense does not matter.

God is not oblivious or unfeeling about the gravity of the sins committed against us. For our sake, however, He does not give a pass on forgiveness; He knows the legal right unforgiveness gives the enemy to torment us if we hold on to a debt Jesus Christ already paid. Sometimes it may seem impossible to say the words "I forgive," yet God is a God of the impossible, even in the matter of forgiveness.

I was praying with a client whose life traumas at the hands of others were horrendous. It was difficult to listen to her and maintain my composure as the counselor. The moment came for me to invite her to say, "I forgive." She said she could not do it. It was not a matter of not wanting to. She absolutely could not make her mouth and tongue articulate those two words. We both felt helpless.

On the inside, I was sending up the *Help me, Jesus,* prayer.

I heard the Holy Spirit say, *Ask her if she is willing to ask for grace to forgive.*

Although I had never heard the phrase *grace to forgive*, I recognized the voice of the Holy Spirit. There was no point in waiting. I immediately asked the woman if she would be willing to ask God for grace to forgive. I was glad she did not ask for an explanation of what it was or how it worked. She allowed me to lead her in a brief prayer asking God to give her grace to forgive. I believe when we pray, something happens, so with the next breath I led her in a prayer of forgiveness for the perpetrator of the abuse. She repeated the prayer with no difficulty or hesitation. Before asking for grace, she had not been able physically to speak even the word "I." Now, with the gift of grace, she was able to forgive the perpetrator verbally.

Forgiveness—A Legal Transaction

Forgiveness is not a feeling; it is a legal transaction between God and me. When I forgive, I am getting out of God's seat of judgment. He is the only one who has a right to condemn me or anyone else. When condemnation is present in my heart, it is evidence that I have taken over God's job.

It is the responsibility of a judge to hold the evidence against the offender and rule on the case. When I hold the evidence file on someone, including myself, I am waiting for the person to ask my forgiveness, make restitution or at least show changed behavior. Until then, I continue to withhold forgiveness.

When God forgave me, He destroyed the record of my sins. The blood of Jesus erased the evidence for God's conviction and judgment against me. Jesus gave His life and shed His blood so that I did not have to be punished.

To forgive means I hand God the file on my offender or on myself and vacate His judgment seat. I am allowing God to handle the case, knowing He is a just Judge who values and preserves the evidence and rules according to truth. The debt owed me is now God's responsibility to collect, not mine. I have forgiven it.

Forgiving God and Ourselves

It is difficult to accept the fact that sometimes I need to forgive God. I know that for some, as you read that statement your mind is screaming, *God is perfect! Why would I need to forgive Him?*

Yes, He is perfect. Yet there have been times when it appeared that He did not come through for me (and perhaps for you). I prayed for someone to be healed, and they died. I went out on a limb for God and ended up being ridiculed. A friend's marriage ended in divorce after I had prayed and fasted for them. In terms of forgiveness, perception is as real as reality. In my heart I have determined—made a judgment—that God did not listen or care, but abandoned me. A file is started on God, and every time I am disappointed with Him I add to it, until I have built a case against Him. Forgiveness means I get out of the seat of judgment toward God and hand Him the file.

The fattest file, however, may be the one I have on myself. The file of evidence you and I keep against ourselves is often the most debilitating. I met with an eighty-year-old lady who had been depressed for sixty years. She had been in and out of hospitals and on medication, yet she still was not free. When she had entered college, she had rebelled against her strict Christian upbringing, engaging in sexual activity that would have shocked her parents. Within a few years, she returned to the principles she had been taught, asking God to forgive her. Soon after, she began to experience depression, which was deep, unrelenting and tormenting. Nothing she did helped. No one had an answer. She searched for freedom for sixty years. In the middle of our appointment I asked her a question, and her answer was telling.

"Have you ever forgiven yourself?"

"Why, no, I didn't realize I needed to."

That one revelation brought an end to sixty years of pain. She made a simple statement out loud to God: "God, I forgive myself for my rebellion as a twenty-year-old. I receive forgiveness."

With those simple words, her life changed. She jumped up from her chair, started dancing around the room, hands in the air, huge smile, saying, "I'm free! I'm free! I'm free!" Some time later, I ran into her. She got right in my face, big grin, and said, "I'm still dancing!"

What would be some things you might need to forgive yourself for, to stop the demons from tormenting you at night and disrupting your sleep? Who would be some people you need to forgive? Before reading any farther, you might want to take a little time and ask God to show you if there is anyone you need to forgive—father, mother, ancestors, spouse, children, friends, co-workers, teachers, pastors, yourself or perhaps God Himself. Allow God to show you any files you have on any of these people, and then one by one, take each file, hand it over to God and forgive them, allowing Him to handle the case. None of Satan's lies of condemnation have any power against our weapon of forgiveness.

Once all the files have been transferred, you may want to take time to go back over the lies listed in the chart earlier in the chapter. You may be aware of a few others you have believed and need to exchange for truth. Out loud, renounce each lie and make a declaration of the truth. It is helpful to do this at a time and in a place where you will not be disturbed by family, friends or co-workers. Sometimes my car is the best place for solitude and freedom to shout the truth. Don't be surprised if you find yourself wanting to do a happy dance like my eighty-year-old client once she had forgiven herself. Freedom is just a breath away!

The Weapon of Love

The two words *weapon* and *love* seem incongruous together, but in God's economy they are suited to sit side by side. Speaking about Himself, God said His thoughts and ways are not like ours (see Isaiah 55:8). Who would ever allow anyone to kill their only son as payment for the sins of generations of rebellious, ungrateful, reprobate people? Only someone motivated by an inconceivable amount of love. That someone is God. John wrote, "God is love" (1 John 4:8). Jesus demonstrated the expression of that love throughout His three years of ministry on the earth. God loved His lost children of the world so much that He made the ultimate sacrifice, and in doing so took away Satan's power of accusation and condemnation.

By our belief in and acceptance of God's offer of forgiveness through Jesus Christ, we can be reconciled to our heavenly Father. The Good News of the Bible is about reconnection, adoption and acceptance into the family of God. The power of a love that could accomplish this is beyond comprehension (see Ephesians 3:19). It was the outworking of this love that disarmed the principalities and powers, made a public spectacle of them and made us more than conquerors.

It is our relationship with this God of love, our heavenly Father, that gives us power against the enemy's weapon of fear. John also wrote, "Perfect love casts out fear" (1 John 4:18). Jesus said He was never alone because the Father was always with Him (see John 8:29). I have the opportunity of experiencing that same abiding presence of the Father with me. With my omnipotent, omniscient Father, none of Satan's fear tactics can touch me. He may try to torment me through fear, but God's presence of perfect love casts all fear out of my presence.

It may take some time to acclimate to this new paradigm where love, forgiveness and truth rule, and the weapons of the enemy are powerless. The key to success is to live one day at a time, walking hand in hand with the Father, experiencing the safety of His love, the words of truth from His mouth and the power of forgiveness against all offense and condemnation.

If you have not had a good relationship with a father growing up, this may seem like a pipe dream and not even something you want. For you to experience power over the enemy's weapon of fear, it may require taking a risk to believe God is a good Father, as modeled by Jesus, and is safe to trust. If you do not feel you have a relationship with God as your Father, or if it has been a distant one, praying the following prayer out loud will give you an opportunity to establish or deepen that connection.

Prayer

Jesus, thank You for being willing to suffer punishment, humiliation and death as payment for my sins. Father, thank You for loving me so much, even before I was born, that You were willing to let Jesus die on my behalf. Thank You for accepting His sacrifice as payment for all my sins. Thank You that I am forgiven. I forgive myself, and I receive Your forgiveness. I am grateful to be Your child, redeemed, restored and reconciled—no longer an orphan. I desire to grow in my knowledge and experience of Your love, which cancels the power of deception, condemnation and fear. Together with You as my Father, I will win the battle for the night.

Nuts and Bolts of Repositioning

Give us this day our daily bread.

Matthew 6:11

In my quest to take back my night, I had to make some practical changes in my nighttime routine. It was not enough to know how important sleep is, or how to deal with the enemy's tactics. The achievement of a goal does not happen by chance. It is the result of a focused plan executed on a regular basis. The goal of a night of sleep as God envisioned it would need the same disciplined approach.

Words like *routine, discipline* and *habits* are not as thrilling as words like *dreams, encounters* and *revelation*, but we will not experience the last three without practicing the first three. That is because routine, discipline and habits are the nuts and bolts of repositioning ourselves to win the battle for the night. It is romantic to think of being a free spirit—no controls, no limitations, no rules and no boundaries—being like the wind that blows wherever it wants to. It would be difficult to have any kind of stable relationship with someone like that. The occasional random encounter would be exhilarating, but not something to count on experiencing tomorrow.

The good news is that God designed our body for precision function based on regular, repetitive movements. The internal physical regulator is our heart, which pumps at a consistent number of beats per minute. If a doctor takes your pulse, he listens for an irregular, out-of-sync beat, which is not the norm. God fashioned our body to be in tune with the orderliness of the universe, the sun rising and setting, the moon rising and falling. I am not referring to the New Age philosophy of cosmic oneness. The body does have a clock programed for sleeping, breathing, cell reproduction, ovulation. We don't get into deep thought about the fact that all women's bodies function on a monthly cycle. Regularity is so familiar that it is only when the system ceases to be predictable that we realize there is a problem.

God is the most dependable, regular-as-clockwork Being in the universe. It would make sense that everything He has created and everything He does would reflect His nature. He says of Himself, "I am the LORD, I change not" (Malachi 3:6 KJV). The writer of Hebrews corroborated this when he wrote, "Jesus Christ is the same yesterday, today, and forever" (Hebrews 13:8). As children made in His image and likeness, we are most ourselves when we function within a daily life of routine and predictability.

This does not mean *boring*! But routine creates the framework within which all other activities can function. The fact that we know when the sun will come up every day gives us the parameters we need to schedule activities that require light. It does not limit what we do or how we do it, but when we do it. Setting an alarm clock and establishing a daily schedule have the same benefit of creating space for activity.

Roosters used to be the alarm clock for the day's beginning, and the setting sun the curtain call for the end of the day's play. The modernization of civilization with electricity, 24/7 shops, TV, radio and the Internet has made the idea of a specific daytime or nighttime obsolete. If you happen to work in a building with no windows at night, there is no difference for you between working the day shift from 8 to 5 or the night shift from 11 to 7. Overhead lights are the same no matter what time it is. This nonstop supply of power and illumination makes it easy to stay up all night to finish the thriller by Stephen King, or to watch a marathon showing of *NCIS*, or to keep up with the Australian Open even if you live in the States. And then there is Facebook, which is always on, with friends all over the world posting something profound, sad, funny, mind tripping. Facebook knows no night.

It took revelation about sleep and God dreams to make me willing to examine and change my sleeping habits and establish a routine. The two operative words are *change* and *habit*. I usually think of making changes in my habits around January 1, in the annual tradition of making New Year's resolutions. My need for change did not coincide with that ritual, but we can change habits and establish new routines any day of the year. Today is always the day of salvation, and with it came radical changes for me.

What—Go to Bed Earlier?

Yes, "What—go to bed earlier?" was my exclamation when I realized I would need to change my schedule. I felt like I had at age seven, when my parents set my bedtime. At that age, I lived for the day when I could go to bed when I wanted to.

Now here I am an adult, and God is talking to me about a time to go "night-night." Just as my parents knew what I needed at seven years old, God knows what my body, soul and spirit need now, as an adult, so that I am equipped for the day.

Your current life situation may hinder you from making immediate changes in your sleep schedule because of your family and work responsibilities. Nothing in this book is meant to add stress, pressure, anxiety or guilt. The information I present is intended to *reduce* those pressures through relationship with God and His gift of sleep.

God knows what you need and is able to help you find ways to receive His provision. If it seems impossible, just ask His help—impossibility is His specialty.

What—Turn Off the TV?

Yes, I did not just go to bed earlier; I also turned off the TV. I am not sure which change was more difficult. Having been conditioned for years to fall asleep to the sound of my TV friends' voices, I experienced a period of awkward withdrawal.

The transition was easier when the cable company required a new cable box and I was unsuccessful at setting it up. The error box kept beeping "No Signal." After several failed attempts, I gave up. It would be much easier to say no to the temptation of watching TV in bed if there was no cable connection anyway. My Internet was not powerful enough for streaming, so there was no Netflix, either.

I am sure God was relieved that He no longer would need to sit through endless reruns of *Law and Order*, my nightly bedtime lullaby. (Remember, He is always with us.) Yes, I would lie in bed and watch several episodes every night, even if I had seen them several times before. Sometimes I would fall asleep to the sounds of guns and sirens, only to be awakened by the thud of the remote hitting the floor as my sleepy hand released its grip.

God could have disrupted the cable connection or blown the computer circuit on the TV earlier, but He never did. What a demonstration of patience!

Not My iPad and iPhone, Too!

Never having had any interest in going to bed early, I had never read any articles about sleep deterrents. I always wanted to stay awake, not find ways to doze. Now I was Googling how to fall asleep. There are 51.7 million sites for *insomnia* and 833 million entries for *sleep*. I would have to stay up all night for months to do research about how to fall asleep.

It did not take me long, however, to identify a few enemies of sleep I had allowed into my bed. The name of one of them was Facebook. My nightly routine included spending time checking Facebook, the place where all my friends gather to share profound thoughts about their latest Paleo recipe or baby wipe or dating tip. It is also the place where offense, hurt or loneliness hangs out, waiting for an invitation into my bedroom. Why is it that I can go for days seeing innocuous posts from my friends I don't even know well, yet just as I am about to go to bed, up pops a picture of a surprise birthday party for a friend I do know—an event I was not invited to attend? So, within just a few minutes of going to sleep, I now have to work through forgiving my friend for hurting me. The solution to that kind of sleep inhibitor was no more checking Facebook before going to sleep.

My iPhone was always on as well, resting on top of the iPad, which slept with me in bed. For many years, I was responsible for the care of my elderly mother. My phone had to be on day and night. Once my mother moved to heaven, I turned off the phone. It took some time for my body, mind and emotions to get adjusted to the fact that I was not on call. I did not realize

I had not had a peaceful night's sleep for years. I lived day and night waiting for the call that would notify me she was dying or had died. There are seasons in life when the phone or a baby monitor needs to be on. When that season has passed, however, it is good to turn the phone off, or at least turn on the *Do Not Disturb* setting at night.

Really—No Hot Chocolate?

Coffee has never been my drink of choice. I always said that when I grew up, I would drink coffee. So far, nothing has changed in my coffee habits. I hope that is not indicative of my maturity.

Herbal teas never appealed to me either, so I never incorporated chamomile tea into my nightly routine. Instead, hot chocolate was an evening requirement. I looked forward every evening to climbing into bed, turning on *Law and Order* and savoring a mug of delicious hot chocolate.

Not being someone too involved in checking food labels, I had no idea that hot chocolate had caffeine in it. Once I learned this, no more nighttime drink for me. Even though there is less caffeine in hot chocolate than in a cup of coffee, because I am sensitive to caffeine, that nightly drink made it harder for me to fall asleep.

None of these beverages may be part of your bedtime routine, and you may not be a social media or TV fan, either. But there still may be practical things you can do to improve the length and quality of your sleep. We will not all have the same exact bedtime or routine. But saying that does not mean that what studies have shown about the stimulating effects of the iPad LED screen on the brain does not apply to you or me. Our brains are all wired the same way, just as our bodies are all designed to need a certain amount of sleep.

Pillow Talk with the Father

Even more important than the practical changes we make in preparation for sleep are the spiritual habits we establish. It is good to establish a nighttime spiritual routine. Jesus taught His disciples to pray and ask the Father, "Give us this day our daily bread" (Matthew 6:11). The Old Testament records the experience of the Israelites in the wilderness and how they received manna every day from God (Exodus 16:4). Although we treat our body and spirit as if we were a car that only needs a fill-up every week or two, God did not design us like our car. We need daily care and feeding from God to experience life as He intended.

For many couples, their only time to debrief about the day is at night, before they go to sleep. This is a challenge for some who fall asleep as soon as their head hits the pillow. One lady told me she and her husband talk sitting straight up in bed, because if they don't, one or both of them will fall sleep. If you are married, go ahead and have the pillow talk with your spouse, but don't fall asleep till you talk with your Father. He is eager to hear about your day, as any parent would be. He knows how important it is for His children to have resolution in their heart about the events of the day.

A good prayer to start with is the one David said: "Search me, O God, and know my heart" (Psalm 139:23). Sometimes we don't know what is going on in our emotions until we ask the Holy Spirit to show us. This is a much better practice than the unproductive navel-gazing we engage in sometimes.

We talked about forgiveness in the previous chapter, but let me add that it is good to establish a habit of asking the Holy Spirit every night to show us anyone we need to forgive. The answer probably will not involve major grievances. In some ways, those are easier to forgive than the little offenses—the tone of voice someone uses toward you, being ignored while you are talking, someone else drinking the last cup of coffee in the pot. We all become proficient at glossing over some little offenses and saying, "Oh, it's okay; it doesn't matter."

The truth is, it did matter, and it will have a negative effect on us until we take care of it through forgiveness. Solomon said it is "the little foxes that spoil the vines" (Song of Solomon 2:15). The short time it takes to allow the Holy Spirit to do a heart scan is nothing compared to the loss of a night's sleep if we don't make this part of our nightly spiritual routine.

What Am I Worried About?

Worry is something so normal for many of us that we don't even realize we are doing it. The statistics on insomnia show that anxiety (another word for worry) is at the root of sleep disturbance for some people. Finding out from God if we are anxious about anything before we go to sleep is important.

One day God and I had a short conversation. He said, *I don't want you worrying.*

My immediate response was, *I don't worry!*

He asked me to think of something I had complete peace about and compare that sense of peace with some other areas of my life. Doing that, I realized I did worry about more things than I recognized.

Jesus recognized that worry is a common problem. He talked about people's anxiety about food, drink, clothing and life in general. His antidote for this was knowledge of the truth that the Father knows we have these needs (see Matthew 6:25–32).

Remember, the enemy's tactic is to use fear as a disrupter of sleep. It is our relationship with our Father, the God of love, that overcomes the fear. Peter encouraged us as believers to cast all our care on God because He cares for us (see 1 Peter 5:7).

Although my dad was not always the most encouraging person, I remember him sitting on the side of my bed one night as I sobbed uncontrollably with anxiety about a test I had the next day. He assured me that I would do well and that I did not need to worry. If my father was able to calm my fear about a test, how much more will our heavenly Father bring peace to our anxious heart?

Releasing My Body to Rest in Hope

David testified that his flesh rested in hope (see Psalm 16:9). There are millions of people who wish they could say the same thing. For some, the presence of physical pain robs their body of the rest it needs. For others, emotional pain, which affects the body, hinders sleep as well. The body was never meant to be the carrier of disease or pain of any kind, but rather to be a temple of the Holy Spirit. The Scripture says Jesus took not only our sins, but all our sicknesses, grief and pain in His body, and in that exchange we receive not just forgiveness, but physical and emotional healing (see Isaiah 53:4–5). His body took the pain so our body would not have to carry it.

We can release to God any physical or emotional pain as we get into bed. Jesus spoke to sick bodies and said, "Be healed of your affliction" (Mark 5:34). We can speak those same words to our body, freeing it from carrying the burden of any physical pain or sickness. While we sleep, the Holy Spirit, the same Spirit that raised Jesus Christ from the dead, will be at work bringing healing.

Cultivating an attitude of hope is a key to good rest for our body. God is the God of hope. There is no hope apart from Him. My hope for a good night's sleep and God encounters in the night must rest in Him and not in my new routine or new diet. If we have a history of insomnia, we may need to deal with the dread of another sleepless night. The answer to dread is not in battling, but rather in setting our hope in God.

Hope is the constant expectation of good. When hope is present, there is no room for dread. When hope is present, God is present, because you cannot have hope without God. Hope is the result of a relationship, not an idea or an emotion or a pill we can take and feel better. The fact that the God of hope is also the One who designed us for sleep and gives it to us as a gift is an encouraging truth.

Invitation and Expectation

Once we have gone through our nightly routine, we must still invite God to commune with us while we sleep. God is not a bully. He does not pull rank on us because He is God and we are not. Isaiah said, "The LORD waits to be gracious to you" (Isaiah 30:18 ESV). In the natural, this would be like a parent waiting for a child to ask for help, rather than barging in and taking over because as the parent he or she knows best. God has treasures to give us beyond our wildest dreams, stored up, hidden in the secret place of His pavilion in the darkness. He waits for an invitation into fellowship with us.

We have become so used to people's brash behavior that, often without realizing it, we live within a protective shield. Well-intentioned people who have no manners sometimes invade our space. They may have a great new song or an exciting revelation, and they assume we want to hear it right then. God has good manners. He waits for an open door.

Because I expect God to respond to the open door of my heart, I keep a pen and notebook beside my bed, along with my phone (in silent mode, of course). This equipment adds emphasis to my expectation that He will be visiting me while I sleep. I want to be prepared in case He sings a song that wakens me enough to be able to make a note or a recording. I may have a dream and wake up in the morning aware of all the details, but if I don't write the dream down immediately, I forget some of the pieces of it. Even if I wake up without being aware of a dream or a song from God, I know He has been with me and I have been with Him because I invited Him to spend the night.

David wrote about God's thoughts toward him, "Were I to count them, they would outnumber the grains of sand—when I awake, I am still with you" (Psalm 139:18 NIV). I believe David was aware of the nightly communion between God's Spirit and his spirit while he slept. It would appear that he went to bed aware of God's presence and woke up still in His presence. What a beautiful picture of sweet sleep.

Since I have repositioned myself for the night, I have noticed my prayer time in the morning is different from how it used to be. Sometimes I wake up with an idea for a message, a blog or a book. As soon as I open my journal and begin to write down the idea, it is as if someone takes hold of my pen and suddenly there is an outline for a talk on the page. The notes I make are not the result of a book I have read or a Bible study I have done. I realize God has downloaded these ideas to me as I have slept.

Who knows? You may wake up in the morning with a song, a poem or an invention. God has plenty of treasures stored up—enough for us all.

Prayer

Father, I give You permission to help me adjust my schedule and activities to allow more time for undisturbed sleep. Please remind me every night to forgive any offenses I have toward others and myself. Help me entrust any anxiety and pain to You. Thank You that as I sleep, You are healing my body. You are the source of my hope for peaceful sleep tonight. I can sleep in peace because Your everlasting arms are surrounding me to keep me safe, and when I wake up, You are still with me.

Teach Children to Say "Bye-Bye, Boogeyman"

Let the little children come to Me.

Luke 18:16

We have spent the majority of time in this book addressing the issues of the night that we adults experience. Yet we know that children experience restlessness at night, too, often from nightmares and night terrors, as well as the usual wakefulness from growing pains. Much literature and thousands of studies address the causes and cures of adult insomnia, but many articles do not treat adult insomnia the same as a child's sleeplessness. One example of this is the way we tend to view children's nightmares as "normal" and something they will grow out of.

My experience as a child did not include disturbing nightmares. But I was smart enough at a young age to use nightmares as a way to go and sleep in my parents' bedroom, particularly in the summer. We lived in Texas, and our house was not air-conditioned. The attic fan did not have power to cool the house down at night. Being a four-year-old, I was sent to bed while it was still light and oppressively hot in my room. The only cool room in the house was the master bedroom, which had a window unit.

I came up with a nightmare ruse as a way that I could escape from the heat of my bedroom, into the paradise of my parents' air-conditioned one. I first had to endure several hours of the heat, until I knew my parents were asleep. Then I crept down the hall and put my ear to their door to be certain they were sound asleep before I made my move. The window unit in their bedroom made quite a bit of noise, so it was easy to open their door without being heard and tiptoe across the floor to the chaise lounge in the corner.

I enjoyed this oasis of comfort until my parents noticed that I was making myself a little bed on the chaise, laying down a soft coverlet and pillow, *before* I went to bed in my own room. They then realized my "nightmares" were a smart little four-year-old's pretext for getting out of the heat. Yes, that was the end of my cool nights in the AC.

Children and Nightmares

I am thankful that my nightmares were no more than a ruse to get relief from the heat. But untold numbers of children do have real nightmares and night terrors, which are even more intense than the nightmares. Night terrors are frightening occurrences that happen when a child (or adult) is asleep. They are so vivid and real that people cry out, scream or sometimes get up and walk around even though they are asleep. Often, there is no memory of the entire event afterward.

Nightmares are usually something that the person wakes up remembering—maybe not all the details, but enough to know something scary happened during sleep. Children who have nightmare experiences talk about them as being scary, involving monsters, zombies or alien beings wielding weapons dripping with blood, chasing them, eating them or some other terrifying description. If the child is from a Christian home, the description may involve the words *demons, evil spirits*, or *Satan*. As I indicated in chapter 8, the word *nightmare* actually means "night demon." If a child says he or she saw a demon in the bedroom at night, it is likely the child is not lying or fantasizing. He or she saw a demon.

These frightening experiences of children confirm the truth that they can experience the supernatural realm, just like adults. That means, of course, that they can also encounter God. If children are encountering the spirit world of demons, they can also connect to God's Kingdom through the Holy Spirit. The key is to teach them about God's supernatural realm, how to connect to it, what to expect and how to disconnect from the demonic realms. The challenge is that sometimes children are more aware of the spiritual realm than their parents. In some cases, the parent and child will be learning together, with the child even teaching the parent as they go along.

Before we talk more about dealing with nightmares and night terrors in children, let's look at some examples of kids who encountered God. These stories are told throughout the Bible, both far back in the Old Testament and into the New Testament. They even reach right up into our present day. Such stories provide an assurance that children can and do experience the Holy Spirit and encounter God in every time, at every age—even before they are born, as was the case with John the Baptist leaping in Elizabeth's womb with the arrival of Mary, the mother of Jesus. Let's start first with the Old Testament story of Samuel hearing God's voice calling to him in the night.

God's Call to the Child Samuel

The story of Samuel is a perfect picture of a child being mentored by an adult in God encounters. The backstory about Samuel involves his mother, Hannah, married to Elkanah, but barren. Elkanah had another wife, Peninnah, who had given birth to children and had mistreated Hannah because she was childless. Hannah begged God to give her a child (see 1 Samuel 1–3).

During an annual visit Elkanah and his family made to the temple in Shiloh, Eli the priest noticed Hannah's anguish. He saw her lips moving but heard no words. Thinking she had been drinking, he confronted her:

> "Must you come here drunk?" he demanded. "Throw away your wine!"
>
> "Oh no, sir!" she replied. "I haven't been drinking wine or anything stronger. But I am very discouraged, and I was pouring out my heart to the LORD. Don't think I am a wicked woman! For I have been praying out of great anguish and sorrow."
>
> "In that case," Eli said, "go in peace! May the God of Israel grant the request you have asked of him."
>
> "Oh, thank you, sir!" she exclaimed. Then she went back and began to eat again, and she was no longer sad.
>
> 1 Samuel 1:14–18 NLT

Nine months later, Hannah gave birth to a boy, naming him Samuel, which means "I asked the Lord for him." Three years later, Hannah and her husband went back to the temple in Shiloh, bringing their weaned toddler with them. It was time for Hannah to fulfill her promise to give him back to God. It is hard for me to imagine the scene in the temple. Eli, an aging priest, in a moment becomes the surrogate parent for this living sacrifice, Samuel. Imagine the tears, the clinging, the ripping apart of this little boy from his mother and father. In our society we might even call it abandonment. It was not abandonment, but rather the dedication of Samuel to God. David said, "Even if my father and mother abandon me, the Lord will hold me close" (Psalm 27:10 NLT).

God was faithful to fulfill those words for Samuel, who, according to 1 Samuel 2:21 (NLT), "grew up in the presence of the Lord." Children are meant to grow up under the care of their parents. And Samuel did. In this case, it was his heavenly Father, not his biological one. Although young, he served in a little linen priest's robe alongside Eli, who instructed him in the temple activities.

One night, sound asleep in the temple, the young boy Samuel heard his name called. Thinking it was the priest, he ran to Eli's bed. It turned out his mentor had not called for him. Samuel went back to bed, only to be awakened two more times. After the third time, Eli realized that God was calling the boy, even though Eli himself had not heard the voice. As Samuel's tutor in spiritual things, Eli told him to go back to bed. If he heard his name again, he was to answer, "Speak, Lord, your servant is listening" (1 Samuel 3:9 NLT). Samuel had never had any supernatural encounters, so he needed to be taught what to do.

When God called Samuel the fourth time that night, the boy knew it was not Eli. This time he responded with, "Speak, Lord, your servant is listening." The Lord proceeded to speak to him, giving him a shocking word about Eli's rebellious sons. Verse 15 of 1 Samuel 3 says that Samuel stayed in bed until morning, fearful because of what God had told him. Even young Samuel knew it was improper to speak negative words about someone else's children, particularly if you are a child and they are adults.

Eli, being sensitive to God, knew Samuel had heard something important from Him during the night. The priest used the event as another training moment for his young disciple. Sensing Samuel's fear, Eli taught him the seriousness of being a steward of God's word. Fear of God must overcome fear of man. Samuel had a choice either to tell Eli what God said, or not tell and be struck dead. Eli insisted, "Tell me everything. And may God strike you and even kill you if you hide anything from me!" (1 Samuel 3:17 NLT). Eli was saying that God would kill Samuel if he did not tell all. Rather harsh training tactics, but they worked. Verse 19 (NLT) says, "As Samuel grew up, the LORD was with him, and everything Samuel said proved to be reliable."

An Unborn Baby Encounters God

Samuel was not the only child who had God encounters. Fast-forward to the New Testament story in Luke 1:41–44 of the virgin Mary, now pregnant, carrying the Son of God in her womb. Perhaps to encourage her cousin Elizabeth, now six months pregnant, as well as to process her own recent life-changing experience, Mary went to visit her cousin. She was not able to text Elizabeth about her own pregnancy. There was no social media where she could post one of those cute scenes with tiny baby booties and a calendar with the due date, announcing the new family member.

The instant Mary walked into Elizabeth's house, her cousin knew through a supernatural word of knowledge that Mary was pregnant with the Son of God. At the same moment, Elizabeth was filled with the Holy Spirit and her six-month-old fetus leapt in the womb.

Elizabeth told Mary, "When I heard your greeting, the baby in my womb jumped for joy" (Luke 1:44 NLT). Too bad Elizabeth was not having an ultrasound to record the baby leaping at the sound of Mary's voice.

Was this activity like other baby kicks, or was the fetus experiencing the impact of the Holy Spirit filling his mother? I choose to believe the latter. From this story, I am convinced it is possible even for the unborn to encounter God.

The Boy Jesus with the Rabbis

Although Mary knew from conception that her baby had a unique destiny, it appears she forgot about it at times, in the daily life of raising a son. Luke 2:42–50 tells the story of the family trip from their home in Nazareth to Jerusalem for the Feast of Passover. In those days, family meant extended family. The feasts were a celebration of God and a time for family reunions. With the crowds, the uniform drab-looking clothing, scarves protecting heads from the wind, dusty tents, it was easy to get lost in the crowd. Everybody looked the same. But parents did not need to have children on a leash for fear of their getting lost or kidnapped by predators. Everyone in the extended family would look out for and correct each other's children.

When the feast ended, Mary and Joseph loaded up and headed back to Nazareth, a seventy-mile trip. In the evening, they realized Jesus was not with them or any of the others in their group. The next morning they turned around and went back to Jerusalem to search for Him. We are so used to modern-day conveniences now—cell phones, missing persons departments at police stations, high-speed cars, trains and buses—that it is hard to imagine the panic Mary and Joseph must have experienced not having access to a phone or car when they lost track of Jesus. Today we would jump in the car, race back to the venue, high-beam flashlights on, accompanied by a volunteer search team, as well as police who would post an AMBER Alert.

Although Jerusalem was a large city with many residents, camels, soldiers and tourists, Jesus' parents found Him the next day. He was not at the local open-air market, shopping or playing. To their shock, they found Him in the Temple, looking and sounding like an adult, conversing with the rabbis. Forgetting His identity and destiny, Mary and Joseph responded like parents with a normal child who had caused worry and inconvenience. Jesus had to remind them of who He was—the Son of God, needing to be about His Father's business.

Once again, here is an example of a child who was more in touch with spiritual things than the parents were. Jesus is not only a model for what our life is to look like as adults, but also a model for our children. It is possible for children to have wisdom beyond their years and a desire to serve God.

Joan of Arc and the Angels

Childhood God encounters did not stop with Jesus. Throughout history there are stories of supernatural events boys and girls have experienced. Thirteen-year-old Joan of Arc, born in 1412, lived in the obscure French village of Domrémy. The daughter of a farmer, she heard the voice of an angel calling to her as she worked in the garden.

Although Joan's parents had not trained her to expect such visitations, the angel continued to interrupt her daily life over the next several years, giving her an assignment from God to assist in securing the crown for the legal heir to the throne of her country. This historic commission came to this teenager on a farm, not a girl in a convent where, in those days, one might expect something so extraordinary.

Joan was so convinced God was speaking to her that she was willing to endure ridicule, rejection, slander and death. The church leaders convicted her of heresy because she believed God had inspired her actions by angelic visitation. She was burned at the stake in 1431.[1]

Jesus and a Two-Year-Old

There are probably thousands of stories that have never been recorded about incredible dreams or encounters little children have had with God and the angels. As parents learn their children's capacity for spirituality and pay attention when their child wakes up in the morning with a wild story about angels and demons, we are hearing more of these untold stories.

In her book *Children and the Supernatural*, Jennifer Toledo describes her first encounter with Jesus when she was two years old. Nighttime had become terror time for her ever since she had met the roosters next door. That first meeting became the source of the torment she felt at night. She was terrified the roosters would come in through her window and peck her. Her parents tried to comfort her. Their words were powerless. Night after night, she would go to bed filled with anxiety, expressed in nonstop crying. Her parents finally decided she would need to work it out and cry it out herself.

Most parents have had that kind of sleepless night at least once, feeling like a bad parent for letting a poor, helpless child cry himself or herself to sleep. Jennifer's parents fought the temptation to rescue her. The end of the story should give hope to all such parents. In the morning, Jennifer greeted them with "Did you guys see Jesus?"

Not what they expected to hear from their daughter. Their response was a dumbfounded "What?"

In the midst of her anguish, as she was all alone, Jesus came into Jennifer's room and sat on her bed, telling her she did not need to worry. He assured her He would stay perched on her bed, watching the window, keeping any roosters out of her room. That night marked the end of her fear of going to sleep.[2] I am thankful that God is not limited by parents' lack of understanding regarding their children's capacity for Him.

The Holy Spirit and a Twelve-Year-Old

Even growing up in a Christian home did not mean I was encouraged to expect God encounters. As a result, I did not seek them. But God is willing and able to make Himself known to whomever, at whatever age. My second encounter with Him was one night at the age of twelve, when I was sick and alone in the bedroom of a small cottage high in the French Alps. (I told you in chapter 2 about my first experience with God when I was eight.) My French teacher and eleven classmates had left me behind to recover while they proceeded on to where they were camping.

The couple living in the house where I had been left spoke little English, and I spoke little French. I had begged my parents to let me go on this trip, and now I wished they had prevailed in telling me no. I was scared and in pain, certain I would die on the mountain and never see them again.

In the midst of my tears, I heard men's voices singing in beautiful harmonies. The longer they sang, the more peace I felt. The room was filled with a warm Presence. I knew I was safe, enveloped in that unknown atmosphere.

Later, I learned a group of priests were camping higher up the mountain. Their voices were the voice of God speaking to me.[3]

Forgiving Yourself

All these stories throughout the centuries, up to the present day, reinforce the words of Jesus when He told the people, "Let the little children come to Me." If, like my parents, you have not prepared your children for God encounters, it is never too late to start. Or you may have a child who experiences nightmares or night terrors and wants to sleep with the light on all night. Perhaps you realize you have dismissed some of the chatter coming from your three-year-old about a "monsta under da bed." You may feel condemnation for exposing your children to a scary movie, or you may feel bitterness toward someone else who opened the door to fear in them. No matter what the regret or guilt, the place to start in training your children is to forgive yourself. It is often easier to forgive others (even God) than it is to forgive ourselves when it involves our children.

Before you continue reading, it might be good to take a few minutes to ask the Holy Spirit if there is anything you need to forgive yourself for concerning your child. You may feel scared to even ask Him, because His answer might stir up even more regret and pain. He cannot fix a problem if we keep it hidden. It would be like a child with a toy he or she broke and feels guilty about. The child might fear punishment if the toy is shown to Dad or Mom. But if it is not brought out from where it has been hidden in the closet, there is no chance it will be fixed.

Don't let fear keep you from receiving the gift of forgiveness. It is not enough that God offers us this gift. We must accept it, taking ownership of it. A friend may buy you a Christmas gift, wrap it up, ship it to you via UPS, but until you pick the package up from your front door and open it up, you have not received it.

If you find it hard to accept this gift of forgiveness, it may be because of a fear you have about the harm done to your child. Sometimes guilt is tied to consequences we believe are irreversible. For example, a child might have nightmares every night after watching a gory movie at home with his or her parents. The fear of the parent is *My child will always be tormented by fear because of what I allowed.* That parental fear is founded in the lie *The effects of trauma are irreversible, and I am responsible.* If a person believes that lie, then receiving forgiveness becomes almost impossible. Only if I know that my child can be set free and healed will it be possible for me to stop punishing myself through unforgiveness.

Healing for Your Child's Trauma

Modern scientific research continues to reveal the miraculous capacity of the brain to heal from trauma, whether big *T* or little *t* trauma. It was once thought that the brain was set in concrete—immovable and unchangeable. This myth added strength to the lie that early childhood wounds are irreversible. Today, state-of-the-art brain scans debunk that myth. The buzzword in brain science is *neuroplasticity*. An article by educational researcher Kenneth Wesson in *Brainworld Magazine* describes it this way:

> Although we cannot regenerate limbs, we can re-invent our brains (and therefore ourselves) through neuroplasticity. . . .
> . . . In neuroscience, brain plasticity refers to the ability of the brain to modify its structures and neural mechanisms. Changes in brain function occur as the brain re-wires itself in response to new demands placed on it by the external environment. Our malleable brains help us thrive by crafting environmentally appropriate strategies. Brain plasticity underlies the brain's extraordinary capacity to learn, unlearn and relearn.[4]

What this means in layman's terms is that input from the external environment can create new pathways in the brain that bypass other pathways damaged through traumatic experiences, whether big or small. In this case, the input would be a combination of prayer, different types of God-inspired material such as music, books, pictures and movies, as well as connection to God Himself.

If you have believed the lie that trauma effects are irreversible, and if you are fearful about the damage done to your child, perhaps you would like to make this declaration right now to express the truth of the brain's God-given capacity to heal:

Thank You, God, for creating my child's brain with a plasticity that enables it to be restored to Your divine design. I renounce the lie that the harm done to my child, whether by me or someone else, is irreparable. Nothing is impossible with You.

Learning to deal with fear and forgiveness is not just an adult lesson. Any principle of life Jesus taught was simple enough for children. It may be important to give your children an opportunity to forgive someone for opening the door to fear, or forgive themselves for being a "scaredy-cat." Only bringing the fear into the light will enable a child to be free of it. Often, children have an easier time letting go of offenses than we do as adults. Given an opportunity to encounter God as the antidote to fear, most kids are eager to connect to Him.

The Power of a Child's Declarations

The list of declarations in the appendix is a helpful teaching tool to use with children. First, give them a simple explanation of the Scriptures associated with the statements, and then, together out loud, make the declarations.

The power of spoken truth is the same whether through the mouth of an adult or a child. One parent told me about the transformation in her adopted daughter's life through making these declarations. The child's biological mother was a cocaine addict, so from birth as a "crack baby" this girl experienced anxiety at night, needed a light on and took prescription drugs to sleep.

Her adoptive mother brought her to a meeting where I taught about taking back the night. The young girl stood with the audience to make the declarations. She went to bed that night and slept, waking up just once. Over the next several weeks she continued to sleep through the night without needing the light, and her doctor took her off prescription sleep medication.

Ten Truths about Children

The truth that your son or daughter can connect with God as easily as an adult—sometimes more easily—is just one of a number of facts we need to know about kids. Here are ten principles important to believe about children. (Even if you are not a parent yourself, some of these will be applicable to you and the children with whom you may have influence.)

- We as parents have authority, as well as responsibility, concerning our children's spiritual life. We don't need to go to parenting school and earn a parenting certificate to have that authority.
- We as parents have more influence than teachers, preachers or counselors as teachers of our children.
- Children have fewer filters and defenses against God and the spiritual dimension of His nature. They have had less time to develop them than we adults have had.
- The Holy Spirit in your child is the same Holy Spirit in you if you are a believer, and the same Holy Spirit who was in Jesus when He was on earth.
- A child has as much authority over a night demon as you do. We need to teach children to use their authority.
- A baby in the womb can experience the Holy Spirit.
- Children can be taught, just as Samuel was, to know the voice of God and respond to Him.

- God can give destiny dreams to children. Remember, Joan of Arc was a teenager when an angel gave her specific instructions about saving her nation, France. Your child's crazy dreams just may be the call of God on his or her future. Our job is to listen, in order to help our child steward a prophetic word.
- Instead of trying to protect children through isolation, we need to prepare them to take authority over evil spirits.
- Because of fewer inhibitions or theological hindrances, your children may be more in touch with the supernatural than you are. Don't be jealous. As their parent, you are still needed to create an environment where they can grow in their relationship with God. Their experiences will teach you about the undiscovered territories of God's reality.

A Nighttime Routine for Children

One important part of creating an environment conducive to a child's interaction with God is the bedtime ritual. The National Sleep Foundation encourages a strong routine leading up to bedtime. What you do is not as important as how you do it. There is great power in regular association of activities for children, which aids them in falling asleep on time and in peace.[5] As we saw in the previous chapter, we need to adjust our own pre-sleep activities to ensure good sleep. Remember that the goal of sleep is rest for the body and intimacy with God, something children need as much as adults.

Because sleep is so vital for the development of children's minds and bodies, grant money has funded many studies dealing with this issue. Two results from these studies are significant in establishing a bedtime routine. One fact involves food. Yes, it is true that sugar and carbs will stimulate your child. One study done at Columbia University in New York identified three foods that affected good sleep, depending on how much or how little of a substance was eaten during the day. Saturated fats, sugar and lack of fiber were the robbers.[6] It can be a challenge to exchange your child's consumption of candy and chips for nonsugary, high-fiber foods, but the payoff for them and for you could be worth it.

The other finding involved social media. The results of a study conducted by the University of Pittsburgh School of Medicine indicated a direct correlation between sleep and the amount of time young adults devoted to interacting with social media such as Facebook, YouTube, Twitter, Google Plus, Instagram, Snapchat, Reddit, Tumblr, Pinterest, Vine and LinkedIn.[7] The study found that the more time participants spent on social media, the more sleep disturbances they experienced, as compared to their peers in the study who spent less time on social media. Sometimes their exposure to a social media post caused a negative reaction. Anger, rejection and jealousy are a few of the possible emotional responses to a post. Also, the brightness of the screen light on an iPhone or iPad can interfere with the natural heart rhythms of the body. Because young children now have access to electronic devices, a parent's awareness of these findings is important to help monitor a child's interaction with these devices before going to bed.

Creating an Atmosphere for God Encounters

Establishing a bedtime routine and monitoring food and social media are the cornerstones in the natural for creating an atmosphere for good sleep. In the spiritual, there are other practical steps that will increase your child's capacity for God encounters at night.

- Teach your kids Bible stories about children who had God encounters. These testimonies are meant to create expectation. Tell them, "You can have this type of experience, too."

- Even if you don't believe you "see" or "hear" God that well, ask your children questions to find out what they might already be "seeing" or "hearing." There are times I have been around babies or toddlers who just stare at me, following me with their eyes, sometimes leaving the safety of their parents to interact with me, a stranger. I believe they are "seeing" God's presence or angels around me.

- If your children talk to you about monsters, ghosts, aliens, grotesque animals hiding in the closet or under the bed, do not dismiss it or tell them, "Big boys and girls aren't afraid." If there were a robber in your house, you would be scared and would immediately take action to kick out the intruder. Children need to know they have authority in Jesus' name to get rid of the boogeyman. He is as real in their room as the robber in your house.

- Give kids opportunities to experience the presence of God. This may be in a church, conference or concert setting. It may be in your home or driving in your car on a trip. A mother played one of my instrumental CDs[8] in her car in hopes of quieting her rambunctious kids in the backseat. Within a few seconds of hearing the first track begin, one of her children yelled, "Mommy, Jesus is on the music."

- Encourage your children each night, either with you or by themselves, to ask God if they need to forgive anyone, including themselves. Perhaps they did not do well in school and are angry with the teacher or are feeling like a failure. Teach them the importance of forgiveness in keeping the night demons out of their room. Their unresolved anger is just as much an open door for the enemy as your anger is.

- Leave the kids hugging God when you leave their room. They don't need to feel the physical separation from you negatively if you take them from your arms and put them in the arms of God. They soon learn not to be afraid in the dark, because they feel the security of His arms protecting them.

Prayer

Father, thank You for inviting my children to come to You. Please help me create in them an awareness and excitement about Your presence with them as they sleep. Thank You for the dreams, revelations and songs You have prepared for them at night. It is comforting to know they will sleep in the safety of Your loving arms tonight.

I Had a Dream— Now What?

Let a man regard us in this manner, as servants
of Christ and stewards of the mysteries of God.

1 Corinthians 4:1 NASB

That is a great question! A good night's sleep with a dream is not the final goal. What we do with them should be the focus. Everything we have learned, renounced and prayed in order to take back the night and establish intimacy with God will not fulfill God's purpose if we don't do anything with the treasures He shares with us from the secret place. It would be like receiving a gift of your dream car, only to leave it parked in the garage.

God is purposeful in His giving and never wasteful. Jesus demonstrated this principle in the miracle of the multiplication of the loaves and fishes (see Matthew 14:20). The purpose of the miracle was to feed the multitude, but once everyone was fed, the leftovers were put into baskets for a future use—purposeful stewardship at work.

Remember, Paul told the Corinthians they were called to be faithful stewards of the mysteries of God. His exhortation applies to us as well. The revelations and dreams we receive are part of the vast treasury of mysteries God desires to share with His children. Our job is to pay attention to them. Let's look at several action steps we can take to ensure that God's purpose in giving us the dream is fulfilled.

Value It

Value is the result of a belief system regarding a person, object or event. Our thoughts are influenced both by teaching and revelation. Truth is always a marriage of the truth of the Word and the revelation by the Holy Spirit. Do you remember Abraham Lincoln's dismissal of his dream, which we looked at in chapter 1? His failure to value his dream is evidence of a lack of both the truth of the Word and the revelation by the Holy Spirit. The church of his day believed such events as a dream from God happened in Bible days, but were no longer part of God's communication system.

A second reason for a careless response to dreams is lack of a holy fear of God. At the age of 99, Abraham fell on his face at the appearance of God in a vision (see Genesis 17:3). He was not the only one with that response. Encounters with the glorious presence of God have caused people to fall down, tremble and fear (see Psalm 114:7; Mark 4:41; 5:33). But the erosion of a belief in the all-powerful Lord of Hosts through rationalism results in a casual response to His knock on the door of our heart.

We must remember a God dream is not a figment of our imagination, but comes from the Creator of the universe, the One Job encountered as he was questioned from the whirlwind (see Job 38:1). By the end of God's monologue in Job 38–41, revelation came to Job about just who God is. His response was "I had heard about you before, but now I have seen you with my own eyes" (Job 42:5 NLT).

Protect It

What do you do when you have something of great value? I have a watch my parents gave me when I turned 21. It is valuable because of the occasion and because it was a special birthday gift from my mother and father. It was not a watch I wore playing tennis or cleaning the house.

The closure on the watch did not secure it on my wrist, so I paid a jeweler to add a backup clasp to make sure it did not fall off. All that protection just for a watch, because I valued it.

How much more we need to protect the treasures of God from being lost. But that kind of protection is not as easy as buying a safe or putting an extra clasp on a watchband. The way we keep such treasures safe is to protect our thoughts from the enemy's lies that would rob us through deception.

In 1 Thessalonians 5:8, Paul encourages the believers to put on the helmet of the hope of salvation, a strong defense against the enemy's attack on the mind. We must resist the doubts, insinuations and vain imaginings sent by demons and give them no access to our treasures from the secret place.

Write It Down

One reason people don't remember their dreams is that they don't take the time to make a voice recording, a journal entry or a sketch of them. Daniel knew it was important to preserve a dream or vision. He did not have the benefit of a voice recorder, so he wrote them down, "telling the main facts" (Daniel 7:1).

It is difficult to remember all the details of a dream later, and the details are important. I gain more insight when I can read my notes later and meditate on them with God. God instructed Habakkuk to write the vision that he would be given (see Habakkuk 2:2). A large portion of the Bible is the written record of the revelation that men and women have received from God. They recorded this without the benefit of iPads, MacBook Airs, PCs or even old-fashioned typewriters. I am so glad they did.

Discern the Dream

Without the presence of the Holy Spirit helping us discern the spirits, even the most mature believers can be deceived (see Matthew 24:4). The defeated enemy still roams around trying to rob, kill and destroy. We must remember that his primary weapon is deception, coupled with intimidation. He is a professional pathological liar, and the father of lies (see John 8:44).

Here are some principles of dream discernment that you can use as a template:

1. Is your dream in line with the principles of Scripture?
2. Does it conform to the model of Jesus Christ's character, ministry and teaching?
3. Does it bring you closer to God?
4. Does it bring you closer to other believers, or isolate you from them?
5. Does it bring you encouragement, edification and comfort?
6. Does it confirm other words, Scriptures and counsel you have received?
7. Do other trusted counselors agree it is from God?
8. Does it bring you peace, or pressure and anxiety?

Use Wisdom

Solomon, the wisest man in the world, wrote about wisdom in Proverbs. To him, wisdom was more valuable than gold (see Proverbs 16:16). He concluded wisdom was "the principal thing" and exhorted his readers to "get wisdom" (Proverbs 4:7).

Too bad Solomon was not around to give counsel to Joseph—the Joseph with the coat of many colors. At seventeen, Joseph needed wisdom in sharing the revelation he had received from God while he slept. His dream was about his destiny to rule over his older siblings, and he shared it all with them (see Genesis 37:1–24).

What older brother wants to hear this kind of prophetic word from a kid brother? If I had been one of Joseph's siblings, I might have been resentful, too. Today we would call what Joseph did oversharing. His enthusiasm landed him in a pit and a prison before his promised promotion years later. Wisdom would have helped him keep his mouth shut until God released him to share.

God owns the treasures He reveals, so it is good to get His permission before we reveal them to others.

Get Interpretation from God

It would be better not to have a dream than to have one and miss God's intended meaning. Proper interpretation is as important as discernment. Without the boundaries established by interpretation and discernment, disaster is possible.

I met with a woman who asked for prayer about her marriage problems. She and her husband had married in response to dreams and visions other people had had about them—and had interpreted for them. She told me that a woman in her church had had a dream in which my client, who at the time of the dream was seventeen, was ministering with a young, single man in the same church. The woman with the dream interpreted it to mean that these two young people should marry and minister together. She told my client what she had seen about her, along with her own interpretation.

Another adult had seen the same picture of this young couple in a vision, and he told the young man involved that he felt God was telling the two to marry. The result was that they got married, but they did not live happily ever after! Both the adults assumed that what they saw about this young couple meant they should marry, when in fact it might have meant the two young people would minister together. Big difference!

False assumptions about the meaning of a dream can skew our interpretation of it. So can the lenses through which we view God and other people. If we still see God as the angry God of the Old Testament, that mindset will flavor the meaning we give to a dream. Furthermore, if we have anger or fear active in our life, those emotions will also color our interpretation. We need to ask the Holy Spirit to search our heart and deal with any issues that would hinder our understanding of God's intended meaning.

Pray the Dream

A wise veteran Bible teacher once remarked that prayer is not popular. From his experience, prayer meetings never drew a crowd. There are thousands of books on prayer, and many more thousands of sermons preached on the power and importance of it. Still, prayer is something talked about more than done.

In God's economy, prayer has a high value. Part of the purpose of prayer is to bring about the fulfillment of dreams. The disciples asked Jesus to teach them to pray, and He taught them what we now call the Lord's Prayer. Contained within it are these words: "Your Kingdom come. Your will be done on earth as it is in heaven" (Matthew 6:10). God's intention is that knowledge of Him will cover the earth "as the waters cover the sea" (Isaiah 11:9). As we pray and make declarations in hope on a regular basis, in time that dream will become a reality.

Prayer brings us closer to this fulfillment, and also helps us become more invested in it. True intercession, as opposed to intercession as a religious exercise, moves us from earth to the heavenly prayer meeting via the Holy Spirit. This is a gathering 24/7, led by Jesus, under the direction of the Father, empowered by the Holy Spirit (see Hebrews 7:25). The invitation is an eternal one to whoever wants to participate. Some church prayer meetings may have few attendees; the one in heaven is standing room only.

Jesus taught the disciples more about prayer than just what we find in the Lord's Prayer. He told them they would receive the things they desired if they asked in faith (see Mark 11:24). The intensity of our passion will determine the time we invest in prayer. As we value and protect the dreams we have, we add fuel to the fire that brings them to fruition. This fire of desire becomes the power of prayer and the promise of fulfillment.

Pray the Dream as a Community

We are encouraged to pray as individuals, but also as a community. It is helpful to come together and share with others in a church fellowship what the Lord is saying to each of us. As you share together, you may see a similar thread. Often, He is saying the same thing to other people in your community. Until you come together, you may not know the full picture of

God's purposes and plans. It is important to gather as a body of believers to share your dreams.

The Jewish community experienced this principle of a shared dream theme during the 1930s in Germany. Charlotte Beradt, a young woman living during the Nazi regime's rise to power, collected and wrote down dreams that people were recounting to their therapists at the time. These dreams dealt with sociopolitical issues and were often prophetic, revealing future life under Hitler's regime.

Sadly, these dreams were not seen as originating from God as a warning, but rather as coming from within the shared psyche of the German Jews.[1] What if these visions of the night had been shared within the community and seen as a warning from God? Would lives have been saved?

Envision the Dream

The power of visual images is strong. God designed us to be stimulated by the things we see. It makes sense that He would use our gateway of sight through a dream.

It is easier to remember something if we can associate it with a picture. Why do we snap a picture with our phone or camera? The picture will remind us of something significant associated with a person or event. Just as we review the pictures in our photo album, on our iPad or in our phone, we must replay the visual clip of our dream to keep it fresh.

My mother taught me a powerful way to preserve a dream. I had been a born-again Christian longer than she had, but she began to have dreams long before I did. Without being taught what to do with these treasures, she made a habit of drawing simple sketches of what she had seen. One of those drawings was of me as the Statue of Liberty at a time in my life when I was not fully free. She prayed over the picture and lived to see the fulfillment of that freedom in my life.

Wait for It

I don't know anyone who likes to wait for something, myself included. As the pace of life in the twenty-first century becomes faster, patience becomes more challenging.

The word *wait* is used over one hundred times in the Bible. Paul told the Romans to glory in tribulations because they produced patience, which produced experience, which produced hope. From hope we will experience an outpouring of the love of God (see Romans 5:3–5).

Although waiting sometimes seems like a trial, it is important to know it will be worth the wait, so don't give up. God told Habakkuk, "This vision is for a future time. It describes the end, and it will be fulfilled. If it seems slow in coming, wait patiently, for it will surely take place. It will not be delayed" (Habakkuk 2:3 NLT).

Give Thanks

We are told to walk by faith and not by sight. Faith is the substance of things hoped for. Hope anchored in God can give thanks in advance.

If our confidence is dependent on the circumstances or other people, it will be hard to maintain, and it becomes impossible to celebrate with thanksgiving. Hope in God is a sure thing. He is the same yesterday, today and forever.

People and situations change; God does not. If He gives us a dream about something that will happen in the future to us, to someone else, to our nation, He intends to do His part to bring it to pass.

Be the Dream

We need to be prepared to be the answer to our dreams. A friend told me a dream she had about Africa. In it, she saw believers begging for Bible teaching. She forgot about it until later, when she took a trip to Africa. While there, she was struck by the need for teaching and basic training for new believers—the same thing she had seen in her dream.

This friend went home and began to pray, *Lord, send teachers to Africa!*

One day, God asked her, *Why don't you go?*

Until that day, she had never thought that she could be the one to respond to the cry of the Africans.

Be prepared, because you may be the answer to *your* dream.

Collaborate with God

God never intends to fulfill all the dreams He gives on His own; neither does He expect us to be alone in the process. He set the example of collaboration in Genesis 1 when He said, "Let Us make man in Our image, according to Our likeness" (Genesis 1:26). From the beginning, God revealed Himself as three in one: Father, Son and Holy Spirit. He did not function alone in the work of creation, the fulfilling of His dream of the Garden of Eden.

This principle is a thread throughout the entire Bible. From Moses to Jesus, God has wanted to partner with His children. Moses did not want to go into the Promised Land if the presence of God did not accompany him (see Exodus 33:15). Jesus told the disciples that He was never alone because the Father was always with Him (see John 8:29).

For me, the invitation and exhortation to become like a little child is confirmation that God desires to help me see any dream

He has given me become reality (see Matthew 18:3). One of the chief characteristics of little children is they are always in the presence of their parents or a parent representative. It is a given that children need help learning to tie their shoelaces or ride a bike. We need to put away childishness, but never childlikeness. No matter what our age, Father God wants to hold us by our right hand, accompanying us in every dream adventure (see Psalm 73:23).

Prayer

Father God, thank You for giving me treasures from the darkness while I sleep. With Your help, I will steward these dreams and revelations. Please give me wisdom and patience as I pray over them, working together with You and others, giving You thanks in advance for the fulfillment of each one.

13 Dream Questions

Like most people, you may have questions about dreams. Having begun this journey into the night and the realm of God dreams, you may have even more questions now than when you started. You are not alone. In Googling words related to dreams and dream interpretations, I discovered some startling statistics. There are 894 million websites related to the word *dreams*. A Google search for books about dreams produced a list of 60.8 million references to choose from. There are also 23.8 million sites for the *interpretation of dreams*, the majority of which are not Christian. The point is, people are dreaming and they have questions. In this section I want to respond to some questions you might have.

1. What can I do if I don't remember my dreams?

The comforting answer to this question is the truth that if it is a God dream, the Holy Spirit is able to bring it back to our consciousness because He is the source of all revelation. Paul told the Corinthians that the Holy Spirit takes the things of God and gives them to us (see 1 Corinthians 2:10–12). We just need to ask Him to bring it back to our mind. The dream may not come back right away, but if it was from God and He believes it is important for you to remember, it will come back.

The testimony of Daniel confirms this. He was in a tight spot, his life on the line, because King Nebuchadnezzar demanded the interpretation of his dream without first divulging it. He had told the astrologers, magicians and sorcerers he would cut them in pieces if they were not able to tell him what he had dreamed and then interpret it. Terrified, they politely said his request was impossible. The king's decree to kill all the wise men in Babylon included Daniel and his cohorts. Before the execution, Daniel asked the king for a little time, giving him an assurance the dream would be told and interpreted. The reason for Daniel's confidence was that he knew the same Holy Spirit who gave the dream to the king could give it to him. The Holy Spirit was faithful to do just that, and Daniel's life was spared (see Daniel 2:1–49).

2. I have asked God the meaning of my dream, but I have not heard anything. What should I do?

There are several reasons we are not always able to hear God when we ask Him something. The single most important reason is the mistaken belief that He does not want to talk to us. The teaching many people have grown up with in church is that God speaks to the pastor, who then speaks to the people. The idea is that someone needs special training to have direct communication with God.

This is a carry-over from the Old Testament model of the priest being the intermediary between God and man. Only a select few had this office, or the role of prophet, to speak to the people on God's behalf, as the Holy Spirit would inspire them. After the death, burial and resurrection of Jesus Christ as our representative, the Holy Spirit was sent from the Father on the Day of Pentecost (see Acts 2 and Joel 2). From that moment on, the Holy Spirit was available to all believers as their direct link to God.

Another reason for dullness in our hearing may be lingering guilt or shame. In the majority of my counseling sessions with people, when they ask God the reason they have difficulty hearing or believing Him, His answer is that they don't feel worthy. Usually, this is related to some past sins for which they have not received forgiveness and forgiven themselves.

3. I am still puzzled by a recurring nightmare I had as a child. What should I do?

The first thing to do is ask God whether or not it matters if you have understanding about it. Sometimes our minds hold on to curiosity about things that are unimportant. Paul told the Corinthians that all things were theirs—the world, the present and the future (see 1 Corinthians 3:22). The one thing that was not included was the past, which belongs to God, who is the Alpha and Omega—the beginning and the end.

If God says understanding the recurring nightmare does not matter, then it is time to toss it, asking the Holy Spirit to edit it from your memory. It may have become something the enemy was using either to distract you from the present or to resurrect something from the past that God has taken care of for you.

4. How can I know the difference between a warning dream and one that is sent by the enemy to harass me?

The first test is always the test of peace. Even if God is warning us in a dream, there will be a sense of peace, knowing He is with us, never forsaking us, especially in difficulties. If the peace does not come, then the next step would be to tell the enemy you do not accept the dream and send it back to him marked *return to sender*. If, after you do that, the dream lingers with the same lack of clarity, it would be good to share it with some trusted friends who can pray with you to find out together the source of the dream. Remember the dream my friend had three years before 9/11? She was not sure if the dream was from God, so she shared it with her prayer group and received assurance that it was from Him.

5. Is every dream important, even the "pizza" dreams?

Definitely not! The dreams sent from the enemy in the form of nightmares, or those that nag us with unsettledness and fear, should be rejected immediately. The other dreams may rehash the day or repeat a chance meeting with someone. Yet even if a dream seems mundane, it is always good to ask God if there is anything you need to know from it.

6. How can I tell the difference between a prophetic dream and just a crazy one?

Once again, the key is communication with Father God. Just because something seems crazy does not mean it is not from God. Think about Peter's vision on the roof. He was told in the vision to kill and eat various animals that were forbidden food for a Jew (see Acts 10:9–48). God had to show this vision to him three times, because I am sure Peter thought he was crazy or had been out in the sun too long. Later that day Cornelius, a Gentile, came to his house. The vision then made sense. By law Peter, a Jew, was not supposed to have any contact with someone from another nation or faith. But because of the vision, he knew God was not only giving him permission, but also commanding him to meet with Cornelius. (I am using the example of Peter's vision here, but I think it is applicable even though dreams and visions are two different things. See question 31 for an explanation of the difference between a dream and a vision.)

7. Is it normal for children to have nightmares? I am told it is just developmental. Is there more to it?

Child development books based on secular studies may show that more children than adults have nightmares. The problem is that most of the people writing those books do not know God or what the Word of God says about sleep. Would it make sense for a loving God to include in His divine developmental design nightmares for children? What parent would want that for his or her child? Yet nightmares are considered normal because those doing the studies observe that many children have nightmares. The researchers stop there and conclude it must be normal because of the numbers. The truth is, nightmares are not God's idea of normal! There is sweet sleep for children as well as for adults.

8. If I do something sinful in a dream, have I sinned?

The answer would be no, unless you were sleepwalking and did something illegal in real time, even though you were asleep and thought you were dreaming. (That would be a rare situation, and the jury is still out on the guilt or innocence of a person committing a crime while asleep.) The more important question would be, was God giving you the dream to help you deal with an area of temptation, or was it a dream showing you an area of fear related to that act? It may also be God reminding you of something from the past that He wants to forgive or heal. Once you have asked Him about all those possibilities and have not received any clarity, this may be one of those dreams for which you press "delete."

9. What do I do with a negative dream about myself?

The answer is, talk to Father God. Ask Him, *What do You think about this dream? Is this from You?* It is possible that God may reveal something negative in a dream for the purpose of bringing you freedom in that area—never condemnation. Then ask Him, *What am I to do?* He may tell you to pray the opposite of the dream. He may tell you to do something specific or make a declaration that is the opposite of the dream. He may tell you not to accept the negativity that came with the dream.

10. What do I do when I get a dream about a new believer, and in it God is showing me some sin still in his or her life?

It is just like prophecy, which should edify, exhort and comfort, not tear down, condemn or discourage. The same is true of such dreams. You don't go up to the person and say, "So, I see that you have a problem with porn!" The Holy Spirit will enable you to discover the destiny of the person in the dream.

For example, if you "saw" the person looking at porn at night online in the dream, the Holy Spirit might inspire you to say, "God has destined you to be a person of great faithfulness and purity. You are going to be someone who is safe and able to help others live free from shame."

That kind of approach will require you to hear the Holy Spirit speak to you, particularly if you grew up in a religious church where the typical response might have been to go tell the person, "You should be ashamed; you are married!"

11. What if my dream is scary and makes me afraid?

First, you ask the Holy Spirit if the dream was from God. God does not intend to frighten us. No—just the opposite! If the Holy Spirit says the dream was from God, it will be important to find the root of your fear. Remember, fear is always faith in a lie. God is the God of truth. It is a simple matter of asking Him, *What is the lie I am believing that causes me to be afraid of this dream?* He will show you.

For example, what if you had the dream about 9/11 and were frightened that something terrible was going to happen at your friend's school? You would ask God, *Show me the lie that made me afraid.*

Father God might say, *The lie you are believing is that I will not protect your friend if something bad happens.*

In response, you say, *I renounce the lie that You are not going to protect my friend. What is the truth?*

Then God might answer, *The truth is that everyone will be safe.*

If a dream makes you afraid, God will direct you to reject it, or He will help you find the lie you believe that makes you afraid, so that you can replace it with His truth.

12. What if the dream seems to be something from my past?

This may seem obvious, but the first thing to do is ask the Holy Spirit if the dream came from God. The dream may be so vivid that you find yourself caught up in it before you have a chance to determine the source. If it is from God, the next question is *What do You want me to know or do?* He is the interpreter, as well as the source. If the dream is not from Him, then it goes into the trash, along with any fear, anxiety or guilt associated with it.

13. What if the dream is about something from my past, and I have already dealt with it?

If the dream is from God and there is something He tells you to do in response, this does not mean you did not deal with whatever it was at an earlier time. We are like a diamond with many facets. As we change, walking in a new dimension, there may be a thread from the past that now needs attention. There is no reason to panic. Just let the Holy Spirit help you deal with that newly revealed aspect. Don't feel you need to rehash the whole event from the past.

14. What if the dream shows me being angry with someone?

This may be the Holy Spirit showing some unresolved issue in the relationship. First, it would be good to ask the Holy Spirit if you have any resentment, disappointment or hurt toward the person. If the answer is yes, then forgive him or her right away. Ask God to forgive you for the anger, and if necessary, forgive yourself.

If the Holy Spirit says no, ask if there is anything you need to know about the dream. It may be a warning to be alert and forewarned about an upcoming conversation or event with the person where you might be tempted to become angry. The foreknowledge gives you time to pray for the person, as well as the grace to be able to respond in love.

15. What if the dream shows me something good happening to someone I am close to?

Just because you know the person well does not give you permission to tell him or her the dream. Sometimes the information in the dream is meant to inform your prayers. Your friend, as well as the dream, belongs to God. Even if the dream shows your friend winning the lottery, that information should only be given with God's permission.

16. What if I keep asking and still don't know what the dream means?

There are times when it is important to "hang it on a hook." This means living for a period of time with mystery. We have permission to keep asking, to pray for revelation, to fast in hopes of receiving more clarity, to pray with others for understanding. The temptation is always to give up and devalue a dream if we don't receive the interpretation, even if we believe the dream is from God. Dreams are part of the treasure from God's secret place, which should be valued with no expiration date.

17. What if the dream is tormenting?

Torment is never from God. As a believer, you have the authority to reject any disturbing dream. If you continue to feel harassed by it, the next step is to ask God if there is anyone you need to forgive. Remember the story Jesus told in Matthew 18:23–35 about the man who was imprisoned and turned over to the tormentors because he did not forgive? Torment comes in many forms, and one form is as a nightmare. The way to stop the harassing dream is to forgive quickly and completely anyone God highlights to you.

18. What if the dream is showing me something I am afraid to do?

Fear is always an opportunity to experience the empowering love of God our Father. Our faith is said to work by love (see Galatians 5:6). The faith we need to have in order to obey the dream will be activated through receiving God's love in exchange for our fear. Just because we feel fear does not mean the dream is from the enemy. We can reject, delete, flush the dream over and over, but if it is from God, it will return until we deal with the fear rather than rejecting the dream.

19. Why do some dreams come true, while others don't?

Sometimes we may give up on a dream too soon, not realizing it has a long incubation period. Other times, it may involve a stewarding issue like the story of the bags of money in Matthew

25:14–28. The men who took their money and did something with it, investing it well, received more. The man who buried it through fear had it taken away. God does not need us to accomplish His purposes, but He is inviting our participation here on earth to bring the reality of His Kingdom. He is waiting for us to accept responsibility and fulfill our assignment. When we give up, He may give our assignment to someone else to complete it.

20. What do you do with a dream that does not seem as though it is coming to pass?

If you know the dream is from God, then ask Him, *Is this dream for now?* The dream may be a time-release one. Sometimes we have dreams years before they will ever happen. Just because parts of them have happened and parts have not, it does not mean the dreams were not real and were not from God. It just means the time for their fulfillment has not come. Prayer through the waiting season helps to keep the dream fresh.

21. What do you do with a dream you never get clear interpretation on?

Sometimes if we don't get the interpretation right away, it is because God wants us to share the dream with someone else. I had a counseling session with a woman, and at the end she asked if I would interpret a dream she had had for years and years and years. When she finished, I looked at her and told her that her dream was exactly what we had dealt with in the appointment. It would have been helpful if she had come years earlier for help. God was trying to stir things up in her so she could get healed.

22. How do I learn to discern dreams?

The Holy Spirit living within us enables us to distinguish what is of God. There are four voices we may hear: God's voice, the enemy's, our own and other people's. All four of these voices might influence a dream in one way or another. It is important to cultivate friendship with God so we learn to distinguish His voice from everyone else's. Jesus used the analogy of sheep knowing their shepherd's voice and not following a stranger (see John 10:2–5). It is our relationship with the Lord, who is our Shepherd, that enables us to follow His voice and not all the others.

23. What if I had a dream about someone dying prematurely, and they did? Was I to blame for not doing something to prevent it?

Only God knows the answer to that question. But He is willing to answer, so it is important to ask in order not to be haunted by the dream. If God says you are not responsible, that should settle it. Guilt stemming from false responsibility can open the door to accusation.

If God tells you He showed you the dream so that you would intercede, you may need to ask His forgiveness if you did not obey. Yet even in this situation God does not condemn, and neither should we condemn ourselves. The Bible says, "If we confess our sins, He is faithful and just to forgive us our sins and to cleanse us from all unrighteousness" (1 John 1:9).

24. I have found some websites that will interpret dreams, but it does not sound as if the interpretation is done from a Christian perspective. Would it be okay to let them interpret my dream anyway?

Remember, Daniel said that the interpretation belongs to God (see Daniel 2:28–30). So it would be good to ask God first for the interpretation and then seek counsel from a believer, rather than seeking it from someone who does not know God. This does not mean that non-Christians cannot know truth, but there is a probability that their counsel will be a mixture of God's revelatory truth and human understanding. James encouraged believers to be bold in asking God for wisdom: "If you need wisdom, ask our generous God, and he will give it to you. He will not rebuke you for asking" (James 1:5 NLT).

25. What are some good resources to use to interpret my dreams?

The best resource is the Holy Spirit, along with the Word of God. One helpful book is *The Dictionary of Biblical Imagery* (InterVarsity, 1998) as a companion to the Bible. Sometimes dreams contain symbols that would be meaningful to us if we were more familiar with the symbolism in the Bible. In addition, many Christian books on the market provide lists of what different dream images or colors mean. There is a place for these in our library.

I believe God's heart yearns for His children to ask Him, and keep on asking for His interpretation. He does not get frustrated or impatient with our inquiries. Think how you would feel as a parent if, every time your children had a question about the meaning of something they had seen, they would go to your neighbor or a teacher rather than coming to you for the answer. I imagine there would be a twinge of sadness and disappointment that you were not your children's first choice of someone to discuss important questions with.

26. I went to a psychic once, and without me even asking, she told me a dream I had had and interpreted it. How could she do that?

The test of any word is the test of the *spirit* of the word, not the accuracy of it. The psychic who told you your dream and interpreted it did so by the power of a demonic spirit rather than by revelation from the Holy Spirit. Our life as a believer is meant to be under the power and influence of God's Holy Spirit, not the devil's minions. When a prophetic word is spoken, it is our job as the hearers to discern whether it came from God, the person or a demon. The goal of a demon is to entice us to connect with him rather than with the Holy Spirit. A demon will entice us by a demonstration of power through his own signs and wonders. We are in danger of coming under his influence if we allow ourselves to be impressed with the sign or wonder (in this case the correct recounting of a dream) without first discerning its source. The devil comes disguised as an angel of light and does not wear a nametag saying *Satan*. He is only able to do his work through deception.

27. I have dreams in which I am talking to people I once knew who have died. Was it the people I knew, or was it demons I was talking to?

Part of the answer depends on how you felt in the dream or after it. If you were afraid or experienced other negative emotions, it might have been a nightmare inspired by a demon impersonating the person, in which case it is time to press the "delete" button on the dream.

If it is not a nightmare, then it is possible that it was the person's angel appearing in your dream. There is a story in Acts 12 about Rhoda, a young girl who was with the disciples at Mary's house (the mother of John Mark). They were praying for Peter, who was in prison. An angel had come to the prison to set Peter free, leading him through the dark streets to this house. Peter knocked on the door, announcing his presence. Rhoda, hearing Peter's voice, ran to the others with the news. With disdain, they told her it was his angel because they all knew he was in prison (see Acts 12:13–15). The Bible refers to angels over three hundred times. The early Church had many experiences with angels, so much so that no one thought it strange to attribute the knock at the door to Peter's angel.

There are also some occasions when someone who has moved to heaven may appear, sometimes in a dream. Jesus, along with Peter, James and John, had an encounter on a mountaintop in which Moses and Elijah appeared to them. God, not Jesus or the disciples, initiated this event (see Matthew 17:1–7).

In either of these cases, whether a person or his or her angel appears in a dream, it is important to ask God what He wants you to know through this encounter. Sometimes the person appears in the dream to represent a certain characteristic, or is symbolic of a calling or important life event.

This is a different experience from those that occur when a person seeks to talk with the dead through a medium, psychic or sorcerer. In that case, the demons are impersonating the dead person. Since the devil does not have access to people living in heaven or authority over those who did not die in Christ and are awaiting the Day of Judgment, any "people" who appear as the result of trying to contact the dead through a medium are demons—not the deceased person.

28. I have done everything you suggested to deal with my nightmares, but I am still having them. What am I missing?

In this situation, the most important thing to do is stay rooted in the truth that God's gift to His children is sweet sleep and that Jesus Christ has given us all power and authority over the demons. The enemy wants us to doubt the truth or to enter into lies about ourselves, believing God has abandoned us or is mad and unresponsive. This is an important time to invite trusted Christian friends to pray with you for the fulfillment of God's promise of sleep, for revelation of any way the enemy may have access to your sleep, and for an end to the nightmares.

29. I have done everything you suggested, but I am still experiencing insomnia. Is there anything else I can do?

This situation, just like the previous question about nightmares, requires confidence that there will be an end to the insomnia. Sometimes deliverance from the situation may be a process rather than instantaneous, just as with physical healing. Remember, whenever we pray, something always happens! Even if you had just fifteen minutes more of sleep last night than the night before, give thanks, knowing that God is at work and what He starts, He finishes.

30. I have had a dream about a family member dying prematurely. When I shared it with my mother, she said it was the same dream that her mother had had. This freaked me out.

The first step is to ask God if this dream came from Him. If it did not, you get to hit "delete"! If it did come from Him, then first deal with the fear by finding out the truth from God. Ask Him what lie you believe about this dream. Renounce the lie and ask the Holy Spirit to show you the truth. Once peace has returned, ask God what He wants you to know or do in response to the dream. Remember, God never sends us dreams to torment or confuse us, or to bring dread. The Kingdom of God is always marked by righteousness, peace and joy (see Romans 14:17).

31. What is the difference between a vision and a dream?

The answer to this question is simple, although sometimes it seems confusing when reading the Bible. Often in Scripture a vision occurs during the day, while dreams tend to occur at night. The issue is not the time of day, but rather the state of the person having the experience—are they awake or asleep? A vision is a revelation from God that occurs when a person is awake, whether during the day or at night. There are several references in the Bible to "visions of the night" or "night visions" (Genesis 46:2; Daniel 7:7, 13) and other references to visions that occur during the day (see Daniel 10:7; Luke 1:22; Acts 10:3). A dream, however, occurs while a person is asleep, whether during the day or at night. Both a vision and a dream from God are revelatory.

Unanswered Questions?

My purpose in writing this book has not been to help you learn how to interpret dreams. Rather, we have talked about how to position ourselves to receive dreams and how to seek God for further instructions about what to do with them. But in that process, I realize questions may have come up about dreams, and I have sought to answer some of those questions for you in this chapter. I also realize this is not an exhaustive list of questions.

If you have more questions sparked by reading this book, you may contact me by visiting my website, www.faithblatchford .com, and emailing me. Questions are one of the best ways to gain greater revelation about God. There is no stupid question except the one never asked! I will do my best to answer any other questions you have. On my website you will also find mp3 tracks of my instrumental music that I mentioned earlier as a sleep aid, along with other materials you might find helpful in your journey of discovery about our heavenly Father.

Prayer

Holy Spirit, thank You for leading me into truth as You take the mysteries of God and reveal them to me. Just as a little child learns by asking questions, sometimes an inordinate number of questions, You never tire of answering mine. Father God, thank You that Your desire is to give me wisdom, revelation and understanding in all the areas of my life.

14 Good Night and Sweet Dreams

If you are reading this chapter, it means you made it through the entire book—unless of course you are someone who likes to start at the last chapter to see if the heroine lives happily ever after. Because of my belief in the God of hope, I can assure you that this final chapter of the book is like the piece of chocolate put on your pillow in a beautiful hotel room, which melts in your mouth with a lingering taste of sweetness as you lay your head down on the pillow. Rather than review the last chapters or try and add some profound last word, I have written a prayer that I will continue to pray for you.

Prayer from Me for You

Father, thank You for my friends whose desire for sleep, dreams or revelation led them to this book. I ask You, Holy Spirit, to fulfill every prayer they have prayed at the end of each chapter and guide them as they find practical ways to enjoy the sleep You desire to give each night. May they approach nighttime with hope and anticipation of undisturbed communion with You as You reveal treasures from the secret place. Thank You that You are with them when they go to sleep, and that when they wake up, You will still be with them.

Appendix

DECLARATIONS

I encourage you to make the declarations in this appendix part of your regular nightly routine—even as a family. If you have young children, you might take one declaration a night and discuss it at dinner, making sure your kids understand the meaning of the words they will be saying before they go to bed. It would not take long for young children to memorize all these declarations.

These declarations of truth are not something we say once and never again, like the husband who told his wife that he saw no need to keep telling her he loved her, because he had said it when they got married and nothing had changed. Every time we say God's Word out loud, we are being strengthened because His Word is bread to us. We all need daily bread, and this kind is even gluten free!

Another reason these declarations should be part of our preparation for sleep every night is to remind the enemy of these truths. It is not that he has a short memory; he is simply testing us, trying to find an entry point to rob us of the treasures God wants to give us as we sleep. Our verbalization of the Scriptures is a powerful silencer of his lies.

Nightly Declarations

1. God is so rich in kindness and grace that He purchased my freedom with the blood of His Son and forgave my sins (Ephesians 1:7).

2. The Lord says, "Call on me when you are in trouble, and I will rescue you" (Psalm 50:15 NLT).

3. If I call on the name of the Lord, I will be saved (Romans 10:13).

4. My body is the temple of the Holy Spirit. I was bought with the blood of Jesus. I belong to God (1 Corinthians 6:19–20).

5. Greater is the Holy Spirit who lives in me than any spirit in the world (1 John 4:4).

6. I submit my body, soul and spirit to God. I resist the devil, and he will flee from me (James 4:7).

7. "In peace I will lie down and sleep, for you alone, O LORD, will keep me safe" (Psalm 4:8 NLT).

8. I live in the shelter of the Most High God and will rest in the shadow of Almighty God (Psalm 91:1).

9. God, You are my refuge, my place of safety. I will not be afraid of the terror at night. You are my God. I trust You. You are with me (Psalm 91:2–15).

10. God, You created and own the darkness (Genesis 1:1–5).

11. God, You dwell in the darkness (1 Kings 8:12).

12. God, Your hiding place is in the darkness (Psalm 18:11).

13. God, You have treasures to give me from the secret place (Isaiah 45:3).

14. God, You instruct my heart while I sleep (Psalm 16:7).

15. God, You sing over me while I sleep (Zephaniah 3:17).

16. God, You give me songs while I sleep (Job 35:10).

17. God, I am loved by You, and You give me sleep (Psalm 127:2).

18. "With God all things are possible" (Mark 10:27).

19. "My body rests in safety" (Psalm 16:9 NLT).

20. Death and life are in the power of my tongue (Proverbs 18:21).

NOTES

Chapter 1: What If?

1. Ward Hill Lamon, *Recollections of Abraham Lincoln 1847–1865*, ed. Dorothy Lamon Telillard (Washington, D.C.: Cambridge University Press, 1911), 114–17.

2. Ibid.

3. Abraham Lincoln, "Second Inaugural Address," April 10, 1865, *The Abraham Lincoln Papers* at the Library of Congress, Manuscript Division (Washington, D.C.: American Memory Project), https://memory.loc.gov/mss/mal/mal3/436/436 1300/004.jpg.

4. *The International Standard Bible Encyclopedia* II, ed. James Ore, John L. Nuelsen, Edgar Y. Mullins, Morris O. Evans, and Melvin Grove Kyle, rev. ed. (Grand Rapids: Eerdmans, 1980), 874–75.

5. Robert Moss, *The Secret History of Dreaming* (Novato, Calif.: New World Library, 2009), xxi.

6. Hannah Nichols, "Dreams: Why Do We Dream?" *Medical News Today*, July 31, 2015, www.medicalnewstoday.com/articles/284378.php.

Chapter 3: God's Nighttime Activity

1. Tom Doyle with Greg Webster, *Dreams and Visions: Is Jesus Awakening the Muslim World?* (Nashville: Thomas Nelson, 2012), 64–68.

2. Henry Louis Gates Jr., "Who Was the 1st Black American Millionairess?" *The Root*, June 24, 2013, http://www.theroot.com/articles/history/2013/06/who _was_the_first_black_millionairess/5/.

Chapter 4: Five Historic Encounters with God at Night

1. Aigerim Korzhumbayeva, "Harran: Ancient Crossroads City of Mesopotamia," *Electrum Magazine*, March 2, 2013, http://www.electrummagazine .com/2013/03/harran-ancient-crossroads-city-of-mesopotamia/.

2. *I & II Kings*, vol. 5 of *The Pulpit Commentary*, eds. H. D. M. Spence and Joseph S. Exell (McLean, Va.: MacDonald Publishing Company), 205.

3. *Blue Letter Bible* Lexicon, Strong's H7892, s.v. *"shiyr,"* https://www.blue letterbible.org/lang/lexicon/lexicon.cfm?strongs=H7892&t=KJV.

Chapter 5: My Body Was Designed for Sleep

1. Lawrence Epstein and Steven Mardon, *The Harvard Medical School Guide to a Good Night's Sleep* (New York: McGraw Hill, 2007), 11–15.

2. Björn Rasch and Jan Born, "About Sleep's Role in Memory," *Physiological Reviews* 93, April 2013, http://physrev.physiology.org/content/physrev/93/2/681 .full.pdf.

3. Steven Lockley and Russell Foster, *Sleep: A Very Short Introduction* (New York: Oxford University Press, 2012), 53, 110–11.

4. Rasch and Born, "About Sleep's Role in Memory."

5. Lockley and Foster, *Sleep: A Very Short Introduction*, 53, 110–11.

6. Epstein and Mardon, *A Good Night's Sleep*, 16–18.

7. Ibid., 32–36.

8. Eric J. Olson, M.D., "Lack of Sleep: Can It Make You Sick?," Mayo Foundation for Medical Education and Research, July 30, 2015, http://www.mayoclinic .org/diseases/conditions/insomnia/expert-answers/lack-of-sleep/faq-20057757.

9. Epstein and Mardon, *A Good Night's Sleep*, 5.

10. Francesco Cappuccio, Michelle Miller, and Steven Lockley, *Sleep, Health, and Society: From Aetiology to Public Health* (New York: Oxford University Press, 2010), 51–55.

11. Ibid.

12. Epstein and Mardon, *A Good Night's Sleep*, 38.

13. Cappuccio, Miller, and Lockley, *Sleep, Health, and Society*, 36–37.

14. Ibid., 97.

15. Ibid., 131–32.

16. Ibid., 83.

17. A. M. Williamson and Anne-Marie Feyer, "Moderate Sleep Deprivation Produces Impairments in Cognitive and Motor Performance Equivalent to Legally Prescribed Levels of Alcohol Intoxication," *Occupational Environmental Medicine* 57, no. 10, April 15, 2000, http://oem.bmj.com/content/57/10/649 .full.

18. Matthew Miewski, et al., "Chronic Lack of Sleep is Associated with Increased Sports Injuries in Adolescent Athletes," *Journal of Pediatric Orthopedics* 34, no. 2 (March 2014): 129–33.

19. Cheri Mah, et al., "The Effects of Sleep Extension on Athletic Performance of Collegiate Basketball Players," *Sleep* 34, no. 7 (July 2011): 943–50.

20. Rasch and Born, "About Sleep's Role in Memory."

21. Ibid.

22. Lee Brown, "Can Sleep Deprivation Studies Explain Why Human Adults Sleep?" *Current Opinion in Pulmonary Medicine* 18, no. 6 (November 2012): 541–45.

23. Simone Ritter and Ap Dijksterhuis, "Creativity—The Unconscious Foundations of the Incubation Period," *Frontiers in Human Neuroscience* 8, April 2014, http://journal.frontiersin.org/article/10.3389/fnhum.2014.00215/full.

24. Chiara Cirelli, "Brain Plasticity, Sleep, and Aging," *Gerontology* 58, no. 5 (2012): 441–45.

25. Epstein and Mardon, *A Good Night's Sleep*, 41–42.

26. Julia Dewald, Anne Marie Meijer, Frans Oort, Gerald Kerkhof, and Susan Bögels, "The Influence of Sleep Quality, Sleep Duration and Sleepiness on School Performance in Children and Adolescents: A Meta-Analytic Review," *Sleep Medicine Review* 14, no. 3 (2010): 179–89.

27. Yulong Lian, et al., "Association Between Insomnia, Sleep Duration and Poor Work Ability," *Journal of Psychosomatic Research* 78, no. 1 (January 2015): 45–51.

28. Lisa Genzel, V. I. Spoormaker, Boris Konrad, and Martin Dresler, "The Role of Rapid Eye Movement Sleep for Amygdala-Related Memory Processing," *Neurobiology of Learning and Memory* 122, July 2015, http://www.sciencedirect.com/science/article/pii/S1074742715000118.

29. Julio Fernandez-Mendoza, et al., "Insomnia and Incident Depression: Role of Objective Sleep Duration and Natural History," *Journal of Sleep Research* 24, no. 4 (August 2015): 390–98.

30. Epstein and Mardon, *A Good Night's Sleep*, 251.

Chapter 6: God's Gift of Sleep

1. *Blue Letter Bible* Lexicon: Strong's G25, s.v. "*agapaō*," https://www.blueletterbible.org//lang/lexicon/lexicon.cfm?Strongs=G25&t=KJV.

2. Bin Zhang and Yun-Kwok Wing, "Sex Differences in Insomnia: A Meta-Analysis," *Sleep* 29, no. 1 (January 2006): 85–93.

3. Ibid.

4. American Psychiatric Association, *Diagnostic and Statistical Manual of Mental Disorders*, 5th ed. (Arlington: American Psychiatric Association, 2013), 181–200.

5. Thomas Roth, "Insomnia: Definition, Prevalence, Etiology, and Consequences," *Journal of Clinical Sleep Medicine* 3 (2007): 7–10.

6. Sonia Ancoli-Israel, "The Impact and Prevalence of Chronic Insomnia and Other Sleep Disturbances Associated with Chronic Illness," *American Journal of Managed Care* 12, May 15, 2006, http://www.ajmc.com/journals/supplement/2006/2006-05-vol12-n8suppl/may06-2308ps221-s229.

7. David Katz and Colleen McHorney, "Clinical Correlates of Insomnia in Patients with Chronic Illness," *Archives of Internal Medicine* 158, no. 10 (1998): 1099–1107.

8. Yinong Chong, Cheryl Fryar, and Qiuping Gu, "Prescription Sleep Aid Use Among Adults: United States, 2005–2010," *NCHS Data Brief* no. 127 (August 2013): http://www.cdc.gov/nchs/data/databriefs/db127.pdf.

9. Maria Calem, et al., "Increased Prevalence of Insomnia and Changes in Hypnotics Use in England Over 15 Years: Analysis of the 1993, 2000, and 2007 National Psychiatric Morbidity Surveys," *Sleep* 35, no. 3 (2012): 377–384.

10. My source for this information was the Epocrates medical reference app available through iTunes, http://itunes.apple.com.

11. CBS News, "CDC: Nearly 9 Million Americans Use Prescription Sleep Aids," CBS Interactive Inc., August 29, 2013, http://www.cbsnews.com/news/cdc-nearly-9-millon-americans-use-prescription-sleep-aids.

12. Epocrates on iTunes, http://itunes.apple.com.

13. Dana Hollenbach, Riley Broker, Stacia Herlehy, and Kent Stuber, "Non-Pharmacological Interventions for Sleep Quality and Insomnia During Pregnancy: A Systematic Review," *Journal of Canadian Chiropractic Association* 57, no. 3 (2013): 260–70.

14. National Sleep Foundation, "Sleep & Your Lifestyle: 6 Tips to Build a Better Bedroom," May 2016, https://sleepfoundation.org/video-library.

15. Ibid.

16. National Sleep Foundation, "Insomnia: What Causes Insomnia?," May 2016, https://sleepfoundation.org/insomnia/content/what-causes-insomnia.

Chapter 7: I've Been Robbed

1. Mark Thomas, "Nyctophobia—Scared of the Dark," *HealthGuidance*, www.healthguidance.org/entry/13977/1/Nyctophobia--Scared-of-the-Dark.html.

2. Kashmira Gander, "Why Are We Afraid of the Dark?" *The Independent*, February 22, 2016, http://www.independent.co.uk/life-style/health-and-families/features/why-are-we-afraid-of-the-dark-a6889086.html.

3. Catherine Pearson, "Insomnia Could Be Triggered by Fear of the Dark," *Huffington Post*, June 12, 2012, http://www.huffingtonpost.com/2012/06/12/insomnia-afraid-of-the-dark_n_1588104.html.

4. Mansal Denton, "Why Are We Afraid of the Dark?" *Lifehack*, http://www.lifehack.org/articles/lifestyle/why-are-we-afraid-of-the-dark.html.

5. Mark Luskin, "Notes on the Prince of Darkness: Etymology," *Mark Luskin's Blog*, April 15, 2013, markluskin.blogspot.com/2013/04/notes-on-prince-of-darkness-etymology.html.

6. "Prince of Darkness," Project Gutenberg Self-Publishing Press, www.self.gutenberg.org/articles/Prince_of_Darkness.

Chapter 8: The Enemy's Tactics

1. For further information on this topic, see Jamil Hossain and Colin Shapiro, "The Prevalence, Cost Implications, and Management of Sleep Disorders: An Overview," *Sleep Breath* 6, no. 2 (2002): 85–102.

2. CBS News, "CDC: Nearly 9 Million Americans Use Prescription Sleep Aids," CBS Interactive Inc., August 29, 2013, http://www.cbsnews.com/news/cdc-nearly-9-millon-americans-use-prescription-sleep-aids.

3. National Institutes of Health (NIH), "Any Anxiety Disorder Among Adults," April 2015, http://www.nimh.nih.gov/health/statistics/prevalence/any-anxiety-disorder-among-adults.shtml.

4. Harvard Women's Health Watch, "Anxiety and Physical Illness," Harvard Health Publications, Harvard Medical School, July 2008, http://www.health.harvard.edu/staying-healthy/anxiety_and_physical_illness.

5. NIH, "Any Anxiety Disorder Among Adults."

6. Katja Beesdo, Susan Knappe, and Daniel Pine, "Anxiety and Anxiety Disorders in Children and Adolescents: Developmental Issues and Implications for DSM-V," *Psychiatric Clinics of North America* 32, no. 3 (2009): 483–524.

7. Harvard Women's Health Watch, "Anxiety and Physical Illness."

8. Michael First, "Comorbidity of Depression and Generalized Anxiety Disorder," June 20, 2007, http://www.dsm5.org/research/pages/comorbidityofdepression andgeneralizedanxietydisorder(june20-22,2007).aspx.

9. Sudhansu Chokroverty, *100 Questions and Answers About Sleep and Sleep Disorders*, 2nd ed. (Sudbury: Jones and Bartlett Publishers, 2008): 136–39.

10. Barbara Rothbaum, Edna Foa, David Riggs, Tamera Murdock, and William Walsh, "A Prospective Examination of Posttraumatic Stress Disorder in Rape Victims," *Journal of Traumatic Stress* 5, no. 3, July 1992, http://onlinelibrary.wiley.com/doi/10.1002/jts.2490050309/abstract.

11. American Psychiatric Association, *Diagnostic and Statistical Manual of Mental Disorders*, 5th ed. (Arlington: American Psychiatric Association, 2013), 181–200.

12. Rape, Abuse, and Incest National Network (RAINN), "The Offenders—The Rapist Isn't a Stranger," April 2015, https://www.rainn.org/get-information/statistics/sexual-assault-offenders.

13. Jennie Noll, Penelope Trickett, Elizabeth Susman, and Frank Putman, "Sleep Disturbances and Childhood Sexual Abuse," *Journal of Pediatric Psychology* 31, no. 5, June 2006, http://jpepsy.oxfordjournals.org/content/31/5/469.full.

14. Mark Hughes, "20 Highest Grossing Horror Movies of the Last Two Years," *Forbes Magazine*, October 31, 2014, http://www.forbes.com/sites/mark hughes/2014/10/31/top-20-highest-grossing-horror-movies-of-the-last-two-years /#3f5ca80b7045.

15. Noll, Trickett, Susman, and Putman, "Sleep Disturbances and Childhood Sexual Abuse," 469–80.

16. Brad Davis, "Visual Stimulation in Learning," November 17, 2015, http://www.acceleratedlearningmethods.com/visual-stimulation.html.

17. As quoted in Mike Parkinson's article "The Power of Visual Communication," Billion Dollar Graphics, June 2016, http://www.billiondollargraphics.com /infographics.html.

18. Webroot, "Internet Pornography by the Numbers; a Significant Threat to Society," March 2015, http://www.webroot.com/us/en/home/resources/tips /digital-family-life/internet-pornography-by-the-numbers.

19. Eric Dye, "The Staggering Stats of Pornography," *ChurchMag*, March 27, 2012, http://churchm.ag/porn-stats.

20. Stephanie Pappas, "Porn May 'Shut Down' Part of Your Brain," *Live Science*, April 18, 2012, http://www.livescience.com/19755-porn-shut-visual-brain.html.

21. *Dictionary.com*, s.v. "fantasy," http://www.dictionary.com/browse/fantasy?s=t.

Chapter 9: Weapons to Win the Battle

1. *Blue Letter Bible* Lexicon, Strong's G2607, s.v. "*kataginōskō*," https://www
.blueletterbible.org/lang/lexicon/lexicon.cfm?Strongs=G2607&t=KJV.
2. *Blue Letter Bible* Lexicon, Strong's G930, s.v. "*basanistēs*," https://www
.blueletterbible.org/lang/lexicon/lexicon.cfm?Strongs=G930&t=KJV.

Chapter 11: Teach Children to Say "Bye-Bye, Boogeyman"

1. Kevin Miller et al., "Joan of Arc," *Christian History & Biography* 30, Christian History Institute, https://christianhistoryinstitute.org/magazine/article/joan
-of-arc.
2. Jennifer Toledo, *Children and the Supernatural: True Accounts of Kids Unlocking the Power of God through Visions, Healing, and Miracles* (Lake Mary, Fla.: Charisma House, 2012): 75–77.
3. You can find this full story related in "Where I Go, He Goes," my contribution to *Voices of Revival* (Bethel Church, 2013). See pages 8–9.
4. Kenneth Wesson, "Neuroplasticity," *Brain World*, August 26, 2010, www
.brainworldmagazine.com/neuroplasticity.
5. "Perfecting Your Child's Bedtime Routine," *National Sleep Foundation*, https://sleepfoundation.org/sleep-news/perfecting-your-childs-bedtime-routine
/page/0/1.
6. American Academy of Sleep Medicine, "What You Eat Can Influence How You Sleep," *Science Daily*, January 14, 2016, https://www.sciencedaily.com/releases
/2016/01/160114213443.htm.
7. University of Pittsburgh Schools of the Health Sciences, "Social Media Use in Young Adults Linked to Sleep Disturbance," *Science Daily*, January 26, 2016, https://www.sciencedaily.com/releases/2016/01/160126110759.html.
8. My instrumental CDs or mp3s *Age to Come* vols. 1, 2 and 3 (and my other CDs) are available at www.faithblatchford.com.

Chapter 12: I Had a Dream—Now What?

1. Robert L. Van De Castle, *Our Dreaming Mind* (New York: Ballantine Books, 1994), 32.

INDEX

Faith Blatchford serves at Bethel Church in Redding, California, as a pastoral counselor and travels around the world from there as a conference speaker, teaching on various topics including the prophetic, spiritual warfare, dreams and unlocking creative potential. She is also a regional facilitator-at-large of the International Bethel Sozo ministry. Her desire is to help people encounter the presence of God.

Faith says she was born a "Navy brat," but then her dad became an Episcopal priest, making her a PK (preacher's kid) instead. Although her mother sometimes called her a handful, she says neither the Navy nor the Church was to blame! When she was eight, her dad was diagnosed with cancer and sought both medical treatment and divine healing. As a result, Faith had her first encounter with God at a healing service she attended with her parents. Since that experience, she has had a hunger for more of the presence of God. (And yes, her father was healed.)

Faith majored in religion at a secular college (not the easiest thing, she says) and wrote her senior thesis on "The Challenge of Twentieth-Century Divine Healing." She has been in ministry ever since graduation and has served in various places, including a retreat center, some churches and a Christian school. For more information on her ministry and available resources, visit her online at www.faithblatchford.com.